Chambers

Spanish phrasebook

Andrew Hastings

Fernando Léon Solis

D1638654

Chambers

First published by Chambers Harrap Publishers Ltd 2006
7 Hopetoun Crescent
Edinburgh EH7 4AY

ISBN 0550 10285 X

Editor & Project Manager
Anna Stevenson

Publishing Manager
Patrick White

Prepress
Susan Lawrie
Vienna Leigh

Designed and typeset by Chambers Harrap Publishers Ltd, Edinburgh
Printed and bound by Tien Wah Press (PTE.) LTD., Singapore
Illustrations by Art Explosion

CONTENTS

INTRODUCTION

This brand new English-Spanish phrasebook from Chambers is ideal for anyone wishing to try out their foreign language skills while travelling abroad. The information is practical and clearly presented, helping you to overcome the language barrier and mix with the locals.

Each section features a list of useful words and a selection of common phrases: some of these you will read or hear, while others will help you to express yourself. The simple phonetic transcription system, specifically designed for English speakers, ensures that you will always make yourself understood.

The book also includes a mini bilingual dictionary of around 4,000 words, so that more adventurous users can build on the basic structures and engage in more complex conversations.

Concise information on local culture and customs is provided, along with practical tips to save you time. After all, you're on holiday – time to relax and enjoy yourself! There is also a food and drink glossary to help you make sense of menus, and ensure that you don't miss out on any of the national or regional specialities.

Remember that any effort you make will be appreciated. So don't be shy – have a go!

ABBREVIATIONS USED IN THIS GUIDE

adj	adjective
adv	adverb
f	feminine noun
fpl	feminine plural noun
m	masculine noun
mpl	masculine plural noun
n	noun
pl	plural
prep	preposition
sing	singular
v	verb

PRONUNCIATION

In Spanish, words are pronounced as they are written, so once you master a few simple rules you will be able to read it correctly. There are, of course, regional variations, but here we give what might be called standard European Spanish, which is understood everywhere.

Vowels

a	like the *a* in *father*, but shorter
e	like the *e* in *men*, but slightly longer
i	like *ee* in *seen*, but slightly shorter
o	like the *o* in *hot*
u	like *oo* in *spoon*, but slightly shorter

Consonants

b, v	these are pronounced in exactly the same way. In an initial position, and after **m**, like *b* in *butter*; elsewhere, the lips vibrate, but do not actually close to stop the flow of air
c	before **a**, **o** and **u**, like *ck* in *back*; before **e** and **i**, like *th* in *thing*
d	in an initial position, like *d* in *dead*; elsewhere, like *th* in *that*
g	before **a**, **o** and **u**, like *g* in *gag*; before **e** and **i**, like *ch* in Scottish *loch*

Note that in the combinations **gue** and **gui**, the **u** is silent unless written with a diaeresis (**ü**).

h	always silent
j	like *ch* in Scottish *loch*
ll	similar to *lli* in *million*
ñ	like *ny* in *canyon*
qu	like *ck* in *back*
r	a single tap of the tongue on the ridge behind the teeth
rr	a strongly rolled *r*, Scottish-style
v	see **b**, above
w	only found in loan words, pronounced like **b**; see above
z	like *th* in *thing*

Other consonants (f, k, l, m, n, p, s) are pronounced as in English.

For every sentence written in Spanish in this guide, you will find the pronunciation given in italics. If you follow this phonetic transcription, you will be able to make yourself understood in Spanish. Do bear in mind, though, that this is a simplified system intended to help you produce reasonably understandable Spanish. Some Spanish sounds don't exist in English, and so we have used the following codes to transcribe them.

Remember to stress the syllables in **bold**.

ah	as in *car, father*
air	as in *fair, wear*
aw	as in *cause, paws*
ay	as in *day, sleigh*
ee	as in *tree, flea, field*
eye	as in *I, my, eye*
oh	as in *go, throw, sew, although*
oo	as in *soon, spoon*
ow	as in *cow, how, now*
ch	as in *cheese*
CH	as in Scottish *loch*
RR	a strongly rolled *r*
th	as in *thin, thick*

Alphabet

a	*a*	**j**	*CHoh-ta*	**r**	*eRR-ay*
b	*bay*	**k**	*ka*	**s**	*es-ay*
c	*thay*	**l**	*el-ay*	**t**	*tay*
d	*day*	**m**	*em-ay*	**u**	*oo*
e	*ay*	**n**	*en-ay*	**v**	*oo-bay*
f	*ef-ay*	**ñ**	*en-yay*	**w**	*oo-bay doh-blay*
g	*CHay*	**o**	*oh*	**x**	*ek-ees*
h	*a-chay*	**p**	*pay*	**y**	*ee gree-ay-ga*
i	*ee*	**q**	*koo*	**z**	*thay-ta*

EVERYDAY CONVERSATION

In Spain, people kiss each other on the cheek when saying hello or goodbye and are quick to use the familiar **tú** form of address. In fact, you can use this form with shop assistants, waiters and people you have just met, and to some extent in a professional context. The formal **usted** form is used when speaking to elderly people. Note that this is conjugated like the third person (singular for **usted** and plural for **ustedes**); this is because the word is derived from the expression **Vuestra Merced**, meaning "Your Grace". The **usted** form is more widely used in rural areas and villages than in cities.

Buenos días is used as a greeting from morning until lunchtime (which is late in Spain). **Buenas tardes** is used in the afternoon, until around sunset, and **buenas noches** at night. Although there are no hard and fast rules, you are likely to hear **buenas noches** from about 10pm in summer and as early as 6pm in winter, depending on when it gets dark.

The basics

bye adiós *ad-yohs*
excuse me perdone *pair-doh-nay*
good afternoon buenas tardes *bway-nas **tah**-days*
goodbye adios *ad-yohs*
good evening buenas tardes *bway-nas **tah**-days*
good morning buenos días *bway-nos **dee**-as*
goodnight buenas noches *bway-nas **no**-chays*
hello hola *oh-la*
hi hola *oh-la*
no no *noh*
OK vale *bah-lay*
pardon ¿cómo? *koh-moh*

7

> **please** por favor *paw fa-vaw*
> **thanks, thank you** gracias *grath-yas*
> **yes** sí *see*

Expressing yourself

I'd like ...
quisiera ...
kees-ee-air-a ...

we'd like ...
quisiéramos ...
kee-see-air-am-os ...

do you want ...?
¿quiere ...?
kyair-ay ...

do you have ...?
¿tiene ...?
tee-e-ne ...

is there a ...?
¿hay un ...?
eye oon ...

are there any ...?
¿hay ...?
eye ...

how ...?
¿cómo ...?
ko-moh ...

why ...?
¿por qué ...?
paw kay ...

when ...?
¿cuándo ...?
kwan-doh ...

what ...?
¿qué ...?
kay ...

where is ...?
¿dónde está ...?
don-day es-ta ...

where are ...?
¿dónde están ...?
don-day es-tan ...

how much is it?
¿cuánto es?
kwan-toh es

what is it?
¿qué es?
kay es

do you speak English?
¿habla inglés?
ab-la ing-glays

where are the toilets, please?
¿dónde están los servicios?
don-day es-tan los sair-beeth-yohs

how are you?
¿cómo está?
ko-moh es-ta

fine, thanks
bien, gracias
byen, grath-yas

thanks very much
muchas gracias
moo-chas grath-yas

no, thanks
no, gracias
noh, grath-yas

yes, please
sí, por favor
see, paw fa-vaw

you're welcome
de nada
day nah-da

see you later
hasta luego
as-ta lway-goh

I'm sorry
lo siento
loh syen-toh

Understanding

abierto	open
atención	attention
averiado	out of order
entrada	entrance
libre	free
no ...	do not ...
prohibido aparcar	no parking
prohibido fumar	no smoking
reservado	reserved
salida	exit
servicios	toilets

hay ...
there's/there are ...

bienvenido/bienvenida
welcome

¿le importa que ...?
do you mind if ...?

un momento, por favor
one moment, please

siéntese, por favor
please take a seat

PROBLEMS UNDERSTANDING SPANISH

Expressing yourself

pardon?
¿cómo?
ko-moh

what?
¿qué?
kay

could you repeat that, please?
¿puede repetir por favor?
pway-day re-pe-teer paw fa-vaw

could you speak more slowly?
¿puede hablar más despacio?
pway-day ab-lah mas des-path-yoh

I don't understand
no comprendo
noh kom-pren-doh

I understand a little Spanish
comprendo un poco español
kom-pren-doh oon poh-koh es-pan-yol

I can understand Spanish but I can't speak it
comprendo un poco español pero no lo hablo
kom-pren-doh oon poh-koh es-pan-yol peh-roh noh loh ab-loh

I hardly speak any Spanish
no hablo casi nada de español
noh ab-loh ka-see nah-da day es-pan-yol

do you speak English?
¿habla inglés?
ab-lah eeng-glays

how do you say … in Spanish?
¿cómo se dice … en español?
ko-moh say dee-thay … en es-pan-yol

how do you spell it?
¿cómo se escribe?
ko-moh say es-kree-bay

what's that called in Spanish?
¿cómo se llama eso en español?
ko-moh say yah-ma e-so en es-pan-yol

could you write it down for me?
¿puede escribírmelo?
pway-day es-kri-beer-may-loh

Understanding

¿comprende español?
do you understand Spanish?

significa …
it means …

se lo escribo
I'll write it down for you

es un tipo de …
it's a kind of …

TALKING ABOUT THE LANGUAGE

Expressing yourself

I learned a few words from my phrasebook
he aprendido algunas palabras con mi libro de frases
ay a-pren-dee-doh al-goo-nas pa-lab-ras kon mee lee-broh day fra-ses

I did it at school, but I've forgotten everything
lo estudié en el colegio, pero se me ha olvidado todo
loh es-tood-yay en el ko-leCH-yoh pay-roh say may a ol-bi-dah-doh toh-doh

I can just about get by
me defiendo más o menos
may def-yen-doh mas oh may-nos

I hardly know two words!
no sé casi nada
noh say ka-see nah-da

I find Spanish a difficult language
creo que el español es muy difícil
kray-oh kay el es-pan-yol es mwee di-fee-theel

I know the basics but no more than that
sé lo básico, pero nada más
say loh bas-ee-koh, pay-roh nah-da mas

people speak too quickly for me
la gente habla demasiado deprisa
la CHen-tay ab-la de-mas-yah-doh de-pree-sa

Understanding

me parece que se defiende muy bien
I think you manage very well in Spanish

habla español muy bien
you speak very good Spanish

ASKING THE WAY

Expressing yourself

excuse me, can you tell me where the … is, please?
perdone, por favor, puede decirme dónde está el …?
pair-doh-nay, paw fa-vaw, pway-day de-theer-me don-day es-ta el …

which way is it to …?
¿por dónde se va a …?
paw don-day say ba a …

can you tell me how to get to …?
¿puede decirme cómo se va a …?
pway-day de-theer-may ko-moh say ba a …

is there a … near here?
¿hay un … cerca de aquí?
eye oon … thair-ka day a-kee

could you show me on the map?
¿me lo puede señalar en el mapa?
may loh pway-day sen-ya-lah en el ma-pa

is there a map of the town somewhere?
¿hay un plano de la ciudad?
eye oon plah-noh day la thyoo-dad

is it far?
¿está lejos?
es-ta lay-CHos

I'm looking for …
estoy buscando …
es-toy boos-kan-doh …

I'm lost
estoy perdido/perdida
es-toy pair-dee-doh/pair-dee-dah

Understanding

bajar	to go down
continuar	to follow, to keep going
derecha	right
girar	to turn

izquierda	left
subir	to go up
todo recto	straight ahead

¿va andando?
are you on foot?

está a cinco minutos en coche
it's five minutes away by car

es la primera/segunda/tercera a la izquierda
it's the first/second/third on the left

gire a la derecha en la rotonda
turn right at the roundabout

gire a la izquierda en el banco
turn left at the bank

tome la siguiente salida
take the next exit

no está lejos
it's not far

está a la vuelta de la esquina
it's just round the corner

GETTING TO KNOW PEOPLE

The basics

bad	malo *mah-loh*
beautiful	bonito *bo-nee-toh*
boring	aburrido *a-bu-RRee-doh*
cheap	barato *ba-ra-toh*
expensive	caro *kah-roh*
good	bueno *bway-noh*
great	estupendo *es-too-pen-doh*
interesting	interesante *een-te-re-san-tay*
nice	bonito *bo-nee-toh*
well	bien *byen*
to hate	detestar *de-tes-tah*
to like	gustar *goos-tah*
to love	encantar *eng-kan-tah*

INTRODUCING YOURSELF AND FINDING OUT ABOUT OTHER PEOPLE

Expressing yourself

my name's …
me llamo …
may yah-moh …

what's your name?
¿cómo se llama?
ko-moh say yah-ma

how do you do?
¿cómo está?
ko-moh es-ta

pleased to meet you!
¡encantado!
eng-kan-tah-doh

this is my husband
éste es mi marido
es-tay es mee ma-ree-doh

this is my partner, Karen
ésta es mi pareja, Karen
es-ta es mee pa-ray-CHa, ka-ren

I'm English
soy inglés
soy eeng-glays

we're Welsh
somos galeses
som-os ga-lay-says

I'm from …
soy de …
soy day …

where are you from?
¿de dónde es usted?
day don-day es oos-ted

how old are you?
¿cuántos años tiene?
kwan-tohs an-yohs tyen-ay

I'm 22
tengo veintidós
teng-goh bayn-tee-dos

what do you do for a living?
¿a qué se dedica?
a kay say de-dee-ka

are you a student?
¿eres estudiante?
ay-rays es-too-dyan-tay

I work
trabajo
tra-ba-CHoh

I'm studying law
estudio derecho
es-too-dyoh de-re-choh

I'm a teacher
soy profesor
soy pro-fe-saw

I stay at home with the children
me quedo en casa con los niños
may kay-doh en ka-sa kon los neen-yohs

I work part-time
trabajo a tiempo parcial
tra-ba-CHoh a tyem-poh pah-thyal

I work in marketing
trabajo en marketing
tra-ba-CHoh en mah-ke-ting

I'm retired
estoy jubilado
es-toy CHoo-bee-lah-doh

I'm self-employed
soy autónomo
soy ow-toh-noh-moh

I have two children
tengo dos hijos
teng-goh dos ee-CHohs

we don't have any children
no tenemos hijos
noh te-nay-mos ee-CHohs

two boys and a girl
dos niños y una niña
dos neen-yohs ee oo-na neen-ya

have you ever been to Britain?
¿ha estado alguna vez en Gran Bretaña?
a es-tah-doh al-goo-na beth en gran bre-tan-ya

Understanding

¿es usted inglés?
are you English?

conozco Inglaterra bastante bien
I know England quite well

también estamos de vacaciones aquí
we're on holiday here too

me encantaría ir a Escocia algún día
I'd love to go to Scotland one day

TALKING ABOUT YOUR STAY

Expressing yourself

I'm here on business
estoy aquí de negocios
es-*toy* a-*kee* day ne-*goh*-thyohs

we're on holiday
estamos de vacaciones
es-*tah*-mos day ba-kath-*yoh*-nays

I arrived three days ago
llegué hace tres días
ye-*gay* a-*thay* tres *dee*-as

we've been here for a week
llevamos aquí una semana
ye-*bah*-mos a-*kee* oo-na sem-*ah*-na

I'm only here for a weekend
sólo estamos aquí de fin de semana
soh-loh es-*tah*-mos a-*kee* day feen day se-*mah*-na

we're just passing through
sólo estamos de paso
soh-loh es-*tah*-mos day *pas*-oh

this is our first time in Spain
ésta es la primera vez que venimos a España
es-ta es la pree-*mair*-a beth kay ben-*ee*-mos a es-*pan*-ya

we're here to celebrate our wedding anniversary
estamos aquí para celebrar nuestro aniversario de bodas
es-*tah*-mos a-*kee* pa-ra thel-eb-*rah* nwes-troh a-nee-bair-*sahr*-yoh de *boh*-das

we're on our honeymoon
estamos de luna de miel
es-*tah*-mos day *loo*-na day myel

we're here with friends
estamos aquí con amigos
es-*tah*-mos a-*kee* kon a-*mee*-gohs

we're touring around
estamos visitando la zona
es-*tah*-mos bee-zee-*tan*-doh la *thoh*-na

we managed to get a cheap flight
conseguimos un vuelo barato
kon-se-*gee*-mos oon bway-*loh* ba-*ra*-toh

we're thinking about buying a house here
estamos pensando en comprar una casa aquí
es-*tah*-mos pen-*san*-doh en kom-*prah* oo-na ka-sa a-*kee*

Understanding

¡que lo pasen bien aquí!
enjoy your stay!

¡disfruten del resto de sus vacaciones!
enjoy the rest of your holiday!

¿es la primera vez que viene a España?
is this your first time in Spain?

¿cuánto tiempo se va a quedar?
how long are you staying?

¿le gusta?
do you like it here?

¿ha estado en …?
have you been to …?

STAYING IN TOUCH

Expressing yourself

we should stay in touch
deberíamos seguir en contacto
de-ber-*ee*-a-mos se-*geer* en kon-*tak*-toh

I'll give you my e-mail address
le daré mi e-mail
lay da-ray mee ee-mayl

here's my address, if you ever come to Britain
aquí tiene mi dirección, si alguna vez viene a Gran Bretaña
a-kee tyen-ay mee dee-rek-thyohn, see al-goo-na beth byen-ay a gran bre-tan-ya

Understanding

¿me dice su dirección?
will you give me your address?

¿tiene e-mail?
do you have an e-mail address?

puede venir a quedarse con nosotros cuando quiera
you're always welcome to come and stay with us here

EXPRESSING YOUR OPINION

Expressing yourself

I really like …
me gusta mucho …
*may **goos**-ta **moo**-choh …*

I don't like …
no me gusta …
*noh may **goos**-ta …*

I love …
me encanta …
*may eng-**kan**-ta …*

I would like …
me gustaría …
may goos-ta-ree-a …

I really liked …
me gustó mucho …
*may goos-**toh moo**-choh …*

I didn't like …
no me gustó …
*noh may goos-**toh** …*

I loved …
me encantó …
*may eng-kan-**toh** …*

I would have liked …
me habría gustado …
*may a-**bree**-a goos-**tah**-doh …*

I find it ...
creo que es ...
kray-oh kay es ...

I found it ...
creo que era ...
kray-oh kay air-a ...

it's lovely
es bonito
es bon-ee-toh

it was lovely
fue bonito
fway bon-ee-toh

it's not bad
no está mal
noh es-ta mal

it wasn't bad
no estuvo mal
noh es-too-boh mal

it's boring
es aburrido
es a-boo-RRee-doh

it was boring
fue aburrido
fway a-boo-RRee-doh

I agree
estoy de acuerdo
es-toy day a-kwair-doh

I don't agree
no estoy de acuerdo
noh es-toy day a-kwair-doh

I don't know
no sé
noh say

I don't mind
me da igual
may da eeg-wal

it doesn't appeal to me
no me hace mucha gracia
noh may a-tahy moo-cha grath-ya

it sounds interesting
parece interesante
pa-reth-ay een-tay-ray-san-tay

it really annoys me
me molesta de verdad
may mo-les-ta day bair-dad

it's a rip-off
es un robo
es oon roh-boh

it gets very busy at night
se llena de gente por la noche
say yay-na day CHen-tay paw la no-chay

it's too busy
hay demasiada gente
eye de-mas-yah-da CHen-tay

it's very quiet
está tranquilo
es-ta trang-kee-loh

I really enjoyed myself
me lo pasé muy bien
may loh pa-say mwee byen

we had a great time
lo pasamos muy bien
loh pa-sah-mos mwee byen

there was a really good atmosphere
había muy buen ambiente
a-bee-a mwee bwen am-byen-tay

we met some nice people
conocimos a gente muy simpática
kon-o-thee-mos a CHen-tay mwee sim-pa-tee-ka

we found a great hotel
encontramos un hotel muy bueno
eng-kon-trah-mos oon oh-tel mwee bway-noh

Understanding

¿le gusta ...?
do you like ...?

¿lo pasasteis bien?
did you enjoy yourselves?

recomiendo ...
I recommend ...

no hay demasiados turistas
there aren't too many tourists

no vaya el fin de semana, hay demasiada gente
don't go at the weekend, it's too busy

no es tan bueno como dicen
it's a bit overrated

¿le apetece ...?
do you fancy ...?

debería ir a ...
you should go to ...

es una zona preciosa
it's a lovely area

TALKING ABOUT THE WEATHER

> **Some informal expressions**
> **hace un frío que pela** it's freezing cold
> **hace un tiempo de perros** the weather's foul
> **hace un calor agobiante** it's stifling

what's the weather forecast for tomorrow?
¿cuál es el pronóstico del tiempo para mañana?
kwal es el pro-nos-tee-koh del tyem-poh pa-ra man-yah-na

it's going to be nice
va a hacer buen tiempo
ba a a-thair bwen tyem-poh

it isn't going to be nice
no va a hacer buen tiempo
noh ba a a-thair bwen tyem-poh

it's really hot
hace mucho calor
a-thay moo-choh ka-law

it's really cold
hace mucho frío
a-thay moo-choh free-oh

it gets cold at night
por la noche hace frío
paw la no-chay a-thay free-oh

the weather was beautiful
el tiempo era magnífico
el tyem-poh air-a mag-nee-fi-koh

it rained a few times
llovió algunas veces
yob-yoh al-goo-nas beth-ays

it was raining heavily
llovía mucho
yo-bee-a moo-choh

there was a thunderstorm
hubo una tormenta
oo-boh oo-na taw-men-ta

it's very humid here
hay mucha humedad aquí
eye moo-cha oo-me-dad a-kee

it's been lovely all week
ha hecho muy bueno toda la semana
a e-choh mwee bway-noh toh-da la se-mah-na

we've been lucky with the weather
hemos tenido suerte con el tiempo
ay-mos te-nee-doh swair-tay kon el tyem-poh

Understanding

dicen que va a llover
it's supposed to rain

han previsto buen tiempo para el resto de la semana
they've forecast good weather for the rest of the week

mañana hará calor otra vez
it will be hot again tomorrow

TRAVELLING

The basics

airport	aeropuerto *a-air-oh-pwair-toh*
boarding	embarque *em-bah-kay*
boarding card	tarjeta de embarque *tah-CHay-ta day em-bah-kay*
boat	barco *bah-koh*
bus	autobús *ow-toh-boos*
bus station	estación de autobuses *es-tath-yohn day ow-toh-boos-es*
bus stop	parada de autobús *pa-rah-da day ow-toh-boos*
car	coche *ko-chay*
check-in	facturación *fak-too-rath-yohn*
coach	*(bus)* autocar *ow-toh-kah*; *(on train)* vagón *ba-gohn*, coche *ko-chay*
ferry	ferry *fe-RRee*, transbordador *trans-baw-da-daw*
flight	vuelo *bway-loh*
gate	puerta *pwair-ta*
left-luggage (office)	consigna *kon-seeg-na*
luggage	equipaje *e-kee-pa-CHay*
map	mapa *ma-pa*
motorway	autopista *ow-toh-pees-ta*
passport	pasaporte *pa-sa-paw-tay*
plane	avión *av-yohn*
platform	andén *an-dayn*
railway station	estación de trenes *es-tath-yohn day tray-nes*
return (ticket)	billete de ida y vuelta *beel-yay-tay day ee-da ee bwel-ta*
road	carretera *ka-RRe-tair-a*
shuttle bus	autobús lanzadera *ow-toh-boos lan-tha-dair-a*
single (ticket)	billete de ida *beel-yay-tay day ee-da*
street	calle *kal-yay*
streetmap	callejero *kal-yay-CHair-oh*
taxi	taxi *tak-see*
terminal	terminal *tair-mi-nal*

ticket	billete *beel-yay-tay*
timetable	horario *oh-rah-ree-oh*
town centre	centro de la ciudad *then-troh day la thyoo-dad*
train	tren *trayn*
tram	tranvía *tram-bee-a*
underground	metro *may-troh*
underground station	estación de metro *es-tath-yohn day may-troh*
to book	reservar *re-sair-bah*
to hire	alquilar *al-keel-ah*

Expressing yourself

where can I buy tickets?
¿dónde se compran los billetes?
don-day say kom-pran los beel-yay-tays

a ticket to ..., please
un billete para ..., por favor
oon beel-yay-tay pa-ra ..., paw fa-vaw

I'd like to book a ticket
quisiera reservar un billete
kee-see-air-a res-air-bah oon beel-yay-tay

how much is a ticket to ...?
¿cuánto es un billete para ...?
kwan-toh es oon beel-yay-tay pa-ra ...

are there any concessions for students?
¿hay descuentos para estudiantes?
eye des-kwen-tohs pa-ra es-too-dyan-tays

could I have a timetable, please?
¿me da un horario, por favor?
may da oon oh-rah-ree-oh, paw fa-vaw

is there an earlier/later one?
¿hay uno más temprano/más tarde?
eye oo-noh mas tem-prah-noh/mas tah-day

how long does the journey take?
¿cuánto dura el viaje?
kwan-toh doo-ra el bee-a-CHay

is this seat free?
¿está libre este asiento?
es-*ta lee*-bray es-*tay* as-*yen*-toh

I'm sorry, there's someone sitting there
lo siento, está ocupado
loh *see*-en-toh, es-*ta* o-koo-*pah*-doh

Understanding

billetes	tickets
caballeros	gents
cancelado	cancelled
conexiones	connections
entrada	entrance
información	information
llegadas	arrivals
prohibida la entrada	no entry
retrasado	delayed
salida	exit
salidas	departures
señoras	ladies
servicios	toilets
todos los billetes están agotados	everything is fully booked

BY PLANE

Expressing yourself

where's the British Airways check-in?
¿dónde está el mostrador de British Airways?
don-day es-*ta* el mos-tra-*daw* day *bree*-teesh *eyer*-wayz

I've got an e-ticket
tengo un billete electrónico
teng-goh oon beel-*yay*-tay el-ek-*tron*-ee-koh

one suitcase and one piece of hand luggage
una maleta y una bolsa de mano
oo-na ma-lay-ta ee oo-na bol-sa day mah-noh

what time do we board?
¿a qué hora embarcamos?
a kay aw-ra em-bah-kah-mos

I'd like to confirm my return flight
quisiera confirmar el vuelo de vuelta
kee-see-air-a kon-feer-mar el bway-loh day bwel-ta

one of my suitcases is missing
me falta una de mis maletas
may fal-ta oo-na day mees ma-lay-tas

my luggage hasn't arrived
mi equipaje no ha llegado
mee e-kee-pa-CHay noh a yay-gah-doh

I've missed my connection
he perdido mi conexión
ay pair-dee-doh mee ko-neks-yohn

the plane was two hours late
el avión se retrasó dos horas
el ab-yohn say re-tra-soh dos aw-ras

I've left something on the plane
he olvidado una cosa en el avión
ay ol-vee-dah-doh oo-na koh-sa en el ab-yohn

I want to report the loss of my luggage
quiero denunciar la pérdida de mi equipaje
kyair-oh de-noon-thee-ah la pair-dee-da day mee e-kee-pa-CHay

Understanding

aduana	customs
algo que declarar	goods to declare
control de pasaportes	passport control
embarque inmediato	immediate boarding
facturación	check-in
nada que declarar	nothing to declare
recogida de equipaje	baggage reclaim
sala de embarque	departure lounge
vuelos nacionales	domestic flights

por favor, espere en la sala de embarque
please wait in the departure lounge

¿quiere pasillo o ventana?
would you like a window seat or an aisle seat?

tendrá que hacer transbordo en ...
you'll have to change in ...

¿cuántas maletas tiene?
how many bags do you have?

¿ha hecho usted mismo las maletas?
did you pack all your bags yourself?

¿le ha dado alguien algo para llevar?
has anyone given you anything to take on board?

tiene un exceso de peso de cinco kilos
your luggage is five kilos overweight

aquí tiene la tarjeta de embarque
here's your boarding card

por favor diríjase a la puerta número ...
please proceed to gate number ...

última llamada para ...   **el embarque empezará a las ...**
this is a final call for ...   boarding will begin at ...

puede llamar a este número para ver si su equipaje ha llegado
you can call this number to check that your luggage has arrived

BY TRAIN, COACH, BUS, UNDERGROUND, TRAM

Expressing yourself

can I have a map of the underground, please?
¿me da un mapa del metro?
may da oon ma-pa del may-troh

what time is the next train to …?
¿a qué hora es el próximo tren para …?
*a kay **aw**-ra es el **prok**-see-moh trayn **pa**-ra …*

what time is the last train?
¿a qué hora es el último tren?
*a kay **aw**-ra es el **ool**-ti-moh trayn*

which platform is it for …?
¿de qué andén sale el tren de …?
*day kay an-**dayn sah**-lay el trayn day …*

where can I catch a bus to …?
¿dónde puedo coger un autobús para …?
***don**-day **pway**-doh ko-**CHair** oon ow-toh-**boos pa**-ra …*

which line do I take to get to …?
¿cuál es la línea para ir a …?
*kwal es la **lee**-nay-a **pa**-ra eer a …*

is this the stop for …?
¿ésta es la parada de …?
***es**-ta es la pa-**rah**-da day …*

is this where the coach leaves for …?
¿de aquí sale el autocar para …?
*day a-**kee** sa-**lay** el ow-toh-**kah pa**-ra …*

can you tell me when I need to get off?
¿puede decirme dónde tengo que bajarme?
***pway**-day de-**theer**-may **don**-day **teng**-goh kay ba-**CHar**-may*

I've missed my train/bus
he perdido el tren/autobús
*ay pair-**dee**-doh el trayn/ow-toh-**boos***

Understanding

acceso a los andenes	to the trains
billetes internet	e-tickets
mensual	monthly
reservas	bookings
salida inmediata	tickets for travel today

semanal	weekly
taquilla	ticket office
venta anticipada	advance booking
venta anticipada Internet	Internet bookings

hay una parada un poco más adelante a la derecha
there's a stop a bit further along on the right

sólo importe exacto, por favor
exact money only, please

tendrá que hacer transbordo en ...
you'll have to change at ...

tiene que coger el autobús número ...
you need to get the number ... bus

el tren tiene parada en ...	**a dos paradas de aquí**
this train calls at ...	two stops from here

BY CAR

Spain has a very good road network. Most motorways (**autopistas**, signposted in blue) have tolls, while four-lane highways (**autovías**, signposted in red) are free. The speed limit is 120km/h on both types of road and wearing a seatbelt is compulsory (there are frequent police checks). You can buy **eurosúper** or **sin plomo** (unleaded) petrol and **diesel** at service stations. Taxis are available for hire if they display a green light. They usually charge a supplement for each piece of luggage, as well as on Sundays and bank holidays and after 10pm.

Expressing yourself

where can I find a service station?
¿dónde hay una estación de servicio?
don-day eye *oo*-na es-tath-*yohn* day sair-*beeth*-yoh

lead-free petrol, please
gasolina sin plomo, por favor
ga-soh-**lee**-na seen **plo**-moh, paw fa-**vaw**

how much is it per litre?
¿a cuánto está el litro?
a **kwan**-toh es-**ta** el **lee**-troh

we got stuck in a traffic jam
nos hemos quedado parados en un atasco
nos **ay**-mos kay-**dah**-doh pa-**rah**-dohs en oon a-**tas**-koh

is there a garage near here?
¿hay un garaje por aquí?
eye oon ga-**ra**-CHay paw a-**kee**

can you help us to push the car?
¿nos ayuda a empujar el coche?
nos a-**yoo**-da a em-poo-**CHah** el **koh**-chay

I've broken down
tengo una avería
teng-goh **oo**-na a-bair-**ee**-a

the battery's dead
se ha descargado la batería
say ha des-kah-**gah**-doh la ba-tair-**ee**-a

we've run out of petrol
nos hemos quedado sin gasolina
nos **ay**-mos kay-**dah**-doh seen ga-soh-**lee**-na

I've got a puncture and my spare tyre is flat
tengo un pinchazo y tengo la rueda de repuesto desinflada
teng-goh oon peen-**cha**-thoh ee la roo-**ay**-da day re-**pwes**-toh des-in-**flah**-dah

we've had an accident
hemos tenido un accidente
ay-mos te-**nee**-doh oon ak-thee-**den**-tay

I've lost my car keys
he perdido las llaves del coche
ay pair-**dee**-doh las **yah**-vays del **koh**-chay

how long will it take to repair?
¿cuánto tardará en repararlo?
kwan-toh tah-da-**rah** en re-pa-**rah**-loh

◆ Hiring a car

I'd like to hire a car for a week
quisiera alquilar un coche para una semana
kee-see-air-a al-kee-lah oon koh-chay pa-ra oo-na say-mah-na

an automatic (car)
un coche automático
oon koh-chay ow-toh-ma-tee-koh

I'd like to take out comprehensive insurance
quisiera un seguro a todo riesgo
kee-see-air-a oon say-goo-roh a toh-doh ree-es-goh

◆ Getting a taxi

is there a taxi rank near here?
¿hay una parada de taxis por aquí?
eye oo-na pa-rah-da day tak-sees paw a-kee

I'd like to go to ...
quisiera ir a ...
kee-see-air-a eer a ...

I'd like to book a taxi for 8pm
quisiera reservar un taxi para las ocho de la tarde
kee-see-air-a re-sair-bah oon tak-see pa-ra las o-choh day la tah-day

you can drop me off here, thanks
puede dejarme aquí, gracias
pway-day de-CHah-may a-kee, grath-yas

how much will it be to go to the airport?
¿cuánto cuesta ir al aeropuerto?
kwan-toh kwes-ta eer al a-air-oh-pwair-toh

◆ Hitchhiking

I'm going to ...
voy a ...
boy a ...

can you drop me off here?
¿puede dejarme aquí?
pway-day de-CHah-may a-kee

could you take me as far as …?
¿puede llevarme hasta …?
pway-day ye-bah-may as-ta

thanks for the lift
gracias por el viaje
grath-yas paw el bee-a-CHay

we hitched a lift
fuimos en autoestop
fwee-mos en ow-toh-es-top

alquiler de coches	car hire, car rental
aparcamiento	car park
completo	full *(car park)*
conserve su billete	keep your ticket
libre	spaces *(car park)*
otras direcciones	other directions
prohibido aparcar	no parking
reduzca velocidad	slow
todas direcciones	all directions

necesito su carnet de conducir, documento de identidad, y su tarjeta de crédito
I'll need your driving licence, proof of identity and your credit card

hay una fianza de 300 euros
there's a 300-euro deposit

vale, suba, le llevaré hasta …
all right, get in, I'll take you as far as …

BY BOAT

There are several ferry companies sailing to and from the main Spanish ports. **Transmediterránea** provides a daily service from Barcelona and Valencia to the Balearic Islands, and weekly crossings from Cádiz to the Canary Islands. There is also a service from Santander to Plymouth, which sails from March to September.

Expressing yourself

how long is the crossing?
¿cuánto dura la travesía?
kwan-toh doo-ra la tra-bay-see-a

I'm seasick
estoy mareado
es-toy ma-ray-ah-doh

Understanding

sólo pasajeros de a pie foot passengers only
proxima salida a las ... next sailing at ...

ACCOMMODATION

There are various accommodation options in Spain, but it is best to book ahead, particularly during high season or when there is a festival taking place. **Pensiones**, **casas de huéspedes**, **hostales** and **residencias** all offer good value accommodation (these are essentially the same, that is, small, family-run guest houses). However, prices can vary considerably depending on the season, and may double or even triple in high season. Quality varies too, so make sure you ask to see your room before you accept it. At reception, you'll be asked for some ID and may be required to fill in a form. If you're in the countryside, you might prefer the rural charm of a **casa rural**; these are growing in number and offer the same good value as **hostales**. Hotels (**hoteles**) are more expensive and reservations are essential in high season. **Paradores** are luxury hotels run by the State, many of which are located in beautifully renovated historic sites (old monasteries or castles, for example). Note that hotels, like restaurants, charge 7% **IVA** (VAT), which may not be included in the price advertised.

The basics

bath	baño *ban-yoh*
bathroom	cuarto de baño *kwah-toh day ban-yoh*
bathroom with shower	cuarto de baño con ducha *kwah-toh day ban-yoh kon doo-cha*
bed	cama *ka-ma*
bed and breakfast	pensión *pens-yohn*
cable television	televisión por cable *te-lay-bees-yohn paw kab-lay*
campsite	camping *kam-ping*
caravan	caravana *ka-ra-ba-na*
cottage	casa de campo *ka-sa day kam-poh*
double bed	cama doble *ka-ma doh-blay*
double room	habitación doble *a-bee-tath-yohn doh-blay*
en-suite bathroom	habitación con baño *a-bee-tath-yohn kon ban-yoh*

family room	habitación familiar *a-bee-tath-yohn fa-meel-yah*
flat	piso *pee-soh*, apartamento *a-pah-ta-men-toh*
full-board	pensión completa *pen-syohn kom-play-ta*
fully inclusive	todo incluido *toh-doh ing-kloo-ee-doh*
half-board	media pensión *med-ya pen-syohn*
hotel	hotel *oh-tel*
key	llave *ya-bay*
rent	(noun) alquiler *al-kee-lair*
satellite television	televisión por satélite *tay-lay-bees-yohn paw sa-tay-lee-tay*
self-catering	con cocina propia *kon ko-thee-na prop-ya*
shower	ducha *doo-cha*
single bed	cama individual *ka-ma een-dee-bee-dwal*
single room	habitación individual *a-bee-tath-yohn een-dee-bee-dwal*
tenant	inquilino *een-kee-lee-noh*
tent	tienda *tyen-da*
toilets	servicios *sair-beeth-yohs*
youth hostel	albergue juvenil *al-bair-gay CHoo-be-neel*
to book	reservar *re-sair-bah*
to rent	alquilar *al-kee-lah*
to reserve	reservar *re-sair-bah*

Expressing yourself

I have a reservation
tengo una reserva
teng-goh oo-na re-sair-ba

the name's …
a nombre de …
a nom-bray day…

do you take credit cards?
¿aceptan tarjetas de crédito?
a-thep-tan tah-CHay-tas day kred-ee-toh

Understanding

completo	full
habitaciones libres	vacancies
privado	private
recepción	reception

servicios   toilets

¿me permite su pasaporte, por favor?
could I see your passport, please?

¿puede rellenar este impreso?
could you fill in this form?

HOTELS

do you have any vacancies?
¿tienen habitaciones libres?
tyen-en a-bee-tath-yoh-nays lee-brays

how much is a double room per night?
¿cuánto es una habitación doble por noche?
kwan-toh es oo-na a-bee-tath-yohn doh-blay paw no-chay

I'd like to reserve a double room/a single room
quisiera reservar una habitación doble/individual
kees-yair-a re-sair-bah oo-na a-bee-tath-yohn doh-blay/een-dee-bee-dwal

for three nights
para tres noches
pa-ra tres no-chays

would it be possible to stay an extra night?
¿podría quedarme una noche más?
pod-ree-a kay-dah-may oo-na no-chay mas

do you have any rooms available for tonight?
¿tienen habitaciones para esta noche?
tyen-en a-bee-tath-yoh-nays pa-ra es-ta no-chay

do you have any family rooms?
¿tienen habitaciones familiares?
tyen-en a-bee-tath-yoh-nays fa-meel-yah-rays

would it be possible to add an extra bed?
¿podrían poner una cama supletoria?
pod-ree-an pon-air oo-na ka-ma soo-ple-tawr-ya

ACCOMMODATION

35

could I see the room first?
¿podría ver la habitación primero?
*pod-**ree**-a bair la a-bee-tath-**yohn** pree-**mair**-oh*

do you have anything bigger/quieter?
¿tiene algo más grande/tranquilo?
*tyen-ay **al**-goh mas **gran**-day/trang-**kee**-loh*

that's fine, I'll take it
está bien, me la quedo
*es-**ta** byen, may la **kay**-doh*

could you recommend any other hotels?
¿podría recomendarme otros hoteles?
*pod-**ree**-a re-kom-en-**dah**-may oh-trohs oh-**tel**-ays*

is breakfast included?
¿está incluido el desayuno?
*es-**ta** een-kloo-ee-**ee**-doh el des-eye-oo-noh*

what time do you serve breakfast?
¿a qué hora sirven el desayuno?
*a kay **aw**-ra **seer**-ven el des-eye-**oo**-noh*

is there a lift?
¿hay ascensor?
*eye as-then-**saw***

is the hotel near the centre of town?
¿el hotel está cerca del centro?
*el oh-**tel** es-**ta thair**-ka del **then**-troh*

what time will the room be ready?
¿a qué hora estará lista la habitación?
*a kay **aw**-ra es-ta-**ra lees**-ta la a-bee-tath-**yohn***

the key for room ..., please
por favor, la llave para la habitación …
*paw fa-**vaw**, la **yah**-bay **pa**-ra la a-bee-tath-**yohn** …*

could I have an extra blanket?
¿puede darme una manta más?
*pway-day **dah**-may **oo**-na **man**-ta mas*

the air conditioning isn't working
el aire acondicionado no funciona
el eye-ray a-kon-deeth-yon-ah-doh noh foon-thyoh-na

Understanding

lo siento, estamos completos
I'm sorry, but we're full

sólo tenemos libre una habitación individual
we only have a single room available

¿para cuántas noches es?
how many nights is it for?

¿su nombre, por favor?
what's your name, please?

pueden entrar a partir de mediodía
check-in is from midday

tiene que dejar la habitación antes de las 11 de la mañana
you have to check out before 11am

el desayuno se sirve en el restaurante entre 7:30 y 9:00
breakfast is served in the restaurant between 7.30 and 9.00

¿quiere un periódico por la manana?
would you like a newspaper in the morning?

su habitación no está lista todavía
your room isn't ready yet

puede dejar sus maletas aquí
you can leave your bags here

YOUTH HOSTELS

Spanish youth hostels (**albergues juveniles**) usually impose a curfew.
Prices are not particularly competitive when compared with guest houses.

Expressing yourself

do you have space for two people for tonight?
¿tiene sitio para dos personas para esta noche?
*tyen-ay **seet**-yoh pa-ra dos pair-**soh**-nas pa-ra es-ta no-chay*

we've booked two beds for three nights
hemos reservado dos camas para tres noches
*ay-mos re-sair-**bah**-doh dos **ka**-mas pa-ra tres **no**-chays*

could I leave my backpack at reception?
¿puedo dejar mi mochila en recepción?
*pway-doh de-CHah mee mo-**chee**-la en re-thep-**thyohn***

do you have somewhere we could leave our bikes?
¿hay algún sitio para dejar las bicicletas?
*eye al-**goon** seet-yoh pa-ra de-CHah las bee-thee-**klay**-tas*

I'll come back for it around 7 o'clock
volveré a recogerlo a las 7
*bol-bair-**ay** a re-ko-**CHair**-loh a las **sye**-tay*

the sink's blocked
el lavabo está atascado
*el la-**bah**-boh es-**ta** a-tas-**kah**-doh*

there's no hot water
no hay agua caliente
*noh eye **ag**-wa kal-**yen**-tay*

Understanding

¿tienes tarjeta de socio?
do you have a membership card?

se proporciona la ropa de cama
bed linen is provided

el albergue vuelve a abrir a las 6
the hostel reopens at 6pm

SELF-CATERING

Expressing yourself

we're looking for somewhere to rent near a town
buscamos algo para alquilar cerca de una ciudad
*boos-**kah**-mos **al**-goh pa-ra al-kee-**lah** thair-ka day oo-na thyoo-**dad***

where do we pick up/leave the keys?
¿dónde recogemos/dejamos las llaves?
don-day re-ko-CHay-mos/de-CHah-mos las yah-bays

is electricity included in the price?
¿la electricidad está incluida en el precio?
la el-ek-tree-thee-dad es-ta een-kloo-ee-da en el preth-yoh

are bed linen and towels provided?
¿proporcionan ustedes la ropa de cama y las toallas?
pro-paw-thyoh-nan oo-sted-es la roh-pa day ka-ma ee las toh-al-yas

is a car necessary?
¿hace falta un coche?
a-thay fal-ta oon ko-chay

is there a pool?
¿hay piscina?
eye pees-thee-na

is it suitable for elderly people?
¿está adaptado para personas mayores?
es-ta a-dap-tah-doh pa-ra pair-soh-nas meye-aw-rays

where is the nearest supermarket?
¿dónde está el supermercado más cerca?
don-day es-ta el soo-pair-mair-kah-doh mas thair-ka

Understanding

por favor deje la casa ordenada y limpia antes de salir
please leave the house clean and tidy when you leave

la casa está totalmente amueblada
the house is fully furnished

el precio incluye todo
everything is included in the price

necesitas un coche en esta parte del país
you need a car in this part of the country

CAMPING

It is illegal to camp out in the open, except on specially designated sites. Campsites are generally very large and resemble mini villages, with facilities including a supermarket, swimming pool, disco, bars, restaurants and so on.

Expressing yourself

is there a campsite near here?
¿hay un camping por aquí cerca?
*eye oon **kam**-ping paw a-**kee** thair-ka*

I'd like to book a space for a tent for three nights
quiero reservar un espacio para una tienda para tres noches
*kyair-oh re-sair-**bah** oon es-**path**-yoh pa-ra **oo**-na **tyen**-da pa-ra tres no-chays*

how much is it a night?
¿cuánto es por noche?
kwan-toh es paw no-chay

where is the shower block?
¿dónde están las duchas?
don-day es-tan las doo-chas

can we pay, please? we're at space ...
¿podemos pagar? estamos en el espacio ...
pod-ay-mos pa-gah. es-tah-mos en el es-path-yoh ...

Understanding

son ... por persona por noche
it's ... per person per night

si necesita algo no dude en preguntar
if you need anything, just come and ask

EATING AND DRINKING

In cafés, ask for a **café solo** if you want espresso, otherwise you will be served **café con leche** (a large, milky coffee). A **cortado** is an espresso with a dash of milk, and a **descafeinado** is a decaf. Restaurants usually serve lunch between 1 and 4pm and dinner from 8.30 to 11.30pm. Spaniards tend to have their meals even later than usual in the summer. Water and bread are not always included in the price. Salads are usually served without dressing, and olive oil, vinegar and seasoning are brought separately for you to add yourself. In some restaurants the 7% **IVA** (VAT) is not included and must be added to the bill. It is customary to leave a few coins as a tip, even if service is included.

If you want to go for a drink (**ir a tomar algo**) or for some tapas (**ir de tapas**), bars are open all day and late into the night. Spaniards don't usually stay in one bar for hours, preferring instead to wander round a variety of places, having a drink in one, a snack in the next and so on. Ask for **una caña** for draught beer, **una cerveza** for bottled beer, **una clara** for shandy and **un vino** for a glass of wine (**vino blanco** is white wine and **vino tinto** is red).

Going for traditional **tapas** is a popular pastime all over Spain. **Tapas** are nibbles to enjoy with a drink, or small portions of hot or cold food that can be shared by a group of people. They are usually eaten standing at the bar. You can order from the menu or directly from the counter. There is an infinite variety, so don't hesitate to ask for recommendations. In **tabernas vascas** (Basque tapas bars), which can increasingly be found throughout Spain, customers are given a plate and can make a selection from the bar of the **pinchos** (tapas on a **palillo**, or cocktail stick) on display. The **palillos** must be left on the plate, and are counted up at the end to calculate the number of **pinchos** eaten. See also the **Food and Drink** chapter.

The basics

beer	cerveza *thair-bay-tha*
bill	cuenta *kwen-ta*

black coffee	café solo *ka-**fay** soh-loh*
bottle	botella *bo-**tel**-ya*
bread	pan *pan*
breakfast	desayuno *des-eye-oo-noh*
coffee	café *ka-**fay***
Coke®	Coca Cola® *koh-ka koh-la*
dessert	postre *pos-tray*
dinner	cena *thay-na*
fruit juice	zumo de fruta *thoo-moh day froo-ta*
lemonade	gaseosa *gas-ay-oh-sa*
lunch	almuerzo *al-**mwair**-thoh*
main course	plato principal *pla-toh preen-thee-**pal***
menu	menú *men-oo*
mineral water	agua mineral *ag-wa mee-nay-ral*
red wine	vino tinto *bee-noh teen-toh*
rosé wine	vino rosado *bee-noh ro-**sah**-doh*
salad	ensalada *en-sa-**lah**-da*
sandwich	(with sliced bread) sandwich *san-weech*; (with baguette-style bread) bocadillo *bo-ka-**deel**-yoh*
sparkling	(water) con gas *kon gas*; (wine) espumoso *es-poo-**moh**-soh*
starter	entrante *en-**tran**-tay*
still	(water) sin gas *seen gas*
tea	té *tay*
tip	propina *pro-**pee**-na*
water	agua *ag-wa*
white coffee	café con leche *ka-**fay** kon le-chay*
white wine	vino blanco *bee-noh blang-koh*
wine	vino *bee-noh*
wine list	lista de vinos *lees-ta day bee-nohs*
to eat	comer *kom-air*
to have breakfast	desayunar *des-eye-oo-nah*
to have dinner	cenar *thay-nah*
to have lunch	comer *kom-air*, almorzar *al-maw-thah*
to order	pedir *ped-eer*

Expressing yourself

shall we go and have something to eat?
¿vamos a tomar algo de comer?
bah-mos a to-mah al-goh day kom-air

do you want to go for a drink?
¿quieres ir a beber algo?
kyair-es eer a be-bair al-goh

can you recommend a good restaurant?
¿me recomienda un buen restaurante?
may re-kom-yen-da oon bwen res-tow-ran-tay

I'm not very hungry
no tengo mucha hambre
noh teng-goh moo-cha am-bray

excuse me! *(to call the waiter)*
¡oiga!
oy-ga

cheers!
¡salud!
sa-lood

that was lovely
estaba muy rico
es-tah-ba mwee RRee-koh

could you bring us an ashtray, please?
¿puede traernos un cenicero?
pway-day tra-air-nos oon the-nee-thair-oh

where are the toilets, please?
¿dónde están los servicios?
don-day es-tan los sair-beeth-yohs

Understanding

comida para llevar
takeaway

lo siento, dejamos de servir a las 11
I'm sorry, we stop serving at 11pm

BOOKING A TABLE

Expressing yourself

I'd like to book a table for tomorrow evening
quiero reservar una mesa para mañana noche
kyair-oh res-air-bah oo-na may-sa pa-ra man-yah-na no-chay

for two people
para dos personas
pa-ra dos pair-soh-nas

around 8 o'clock
sobre las ocho
soh-bray las o-choh

do you have a table available any earlier than that?
¿tiene una mesa libre más temprano?
tyen-ay oo-na may-sa lee-bray mas tem-prah-noh

I've reserved a table – the name's ...
he reservado una mesa – a nombre de...
ay res-air-bah-doh oo-na may-sa – a nom-bray day ...

Understanding

reservado
reserved

¿para qué hora?
for what time?

¿para cuántas personas?
for how many people?

¿a qué nombre?
what's the name?

¿fumador o no fumador?
smoking or non-smoking?

¿tiene reserva?
do you have a reservation?

¿le parece bien esta mesa del rincón?
is this table in the corner OK for you?

lo siento, no nos quedan mesas libres
I'm afraid we're full at the moment

ORDERING FOOD

Expressing yourself

yes, we're ready to order
sí, ya hemos elegido
*see, ya **ay**-mos e-le-**CHee**-doh*

no, could you give us a few more minutes?
no, ¿puede darnos un momentito más?
*noh, **pway**-day **dah**-nos oon moh-men-**tee**-toh mas*

I'd like ...
quiero ...
kyair-oh ...

could I have ...?
¿me pone ...?
*may **poh**-nay ...*

I'm not sure, what's "fideuá"?
no sé, ¿qué es la "fideuá"?
*noh say, kay es la fee-day-**wa***

I'll have that
voy a tomar eso
*boy a to-**mah** e-soh*

does it come with vegetables?
¿viene con verduras?
*vyen-ay kon bair-**doo**-ras*

what are today's specials?
¿cuál es la especialidad del día?
*kwal es la es-peth-ya-lee-**dad** del **dee**-a*

what desserts do you have?
¿qué postres tiene?
*kay **pos**-trays **tyen**-ay*

some water, please
agua, por favor
*ag-wa, paw fa-**vaw***

a bottle of red/white wine
una botella de vino tinto/blanco
*oo-na bo-**tel**-ya day bee-noh **teen**-toh/**blang**-koh*

that's for me
eso es para mí
*e-soh es **pa**-ra mee*

this isn't what I ordered, I wanted ...
esto no es lo que yo he pedido, yo quería ...
*es-**toh** noh es loh kay ay pe-**dee**-doh, yoh ke-**ree**-a ...*

could we have some more bread, please?
¿puede traernos más pan, por favor?
pway-day tra-air-nos mas pan, paw fa-vaw

could you bring us another jug of water, please?
¿puede traernos otra jarra de agua, por favor?
pway-day tra-air-nos oh-tra CHa-RRa day ag-wa, paw fa-vaw

Understanding

¿han elegido ya?
are you ready to order?

¿qué quiere de beber?
what would you like to drink?

¿quiere postre o café?
would you like dessert or coffee?

vuelvo dentro de unos minutos
I'll come back in a few minutes

lo siento, no me queda/quedan…
I'm sorry, we don't have any… left

¿estaba todo bien?
was everything OK?

BARS AND CAFÉS

Expressing yourself

I'd like …
quiero …
kyair-oh …

a Coke®/a diet Coke®
una Coca-Cola®/una Coca-Cola® light
oo-na koh-ka koh-la/oo-na koh-ka koh-la leyet

a glass of white/red wine
un vaso de vino blanco/tinto
oon ba-soh day bee-noh blang-koh/teen-toh

a cup of tea
un té
oon tay

a cup of hot chocolate
un chocolate
oon cho-koh-lah-tay

a black/white coffee
un café solo/con leche
oon ka-fay soh-loh/kon le-chay

a coffee and a croissant
un café y un croissant
oon ka-fay ee oon krwa-san

the same again, please
lo mismo, por favor
loh meez-moh, paw fa-vaw

Understanding

sin alcohol
non-alcoholic

¿qué desea?
what would you like?

ésta es la zona de no fumadores
this is the non-smoking area

¿puede pagar ahora, por favor?
could I ask you to pay now, please?

> **Some informal expressions**
>
> **estar pedo** to be pissed
> **tener resaca** to have a hangover
> **estar borracho como una cuba** to be as drunk as a lord

THE BILL

Expressing yourself

the bill, please
la cuenta, por favor
la kwen-ta, paw fa-vaw

do you take credit cards?
¿aceptan tarjetas de crédito?
a-thep-tan tah-CHay-tas day kred-ee-toh

I think there's a mistake in the bill
creo que hay un error en la cuenta
kray-oh kay eye oon aiRR-awr en la kwen-ta

is service included?
¿está incluido el servicio?
es-ta een-kloo-ee-doh el sair-beeth-yoh

how much do I owe you?
¿cuánto le debo?
kwan-toh lay day-boh

Understanding

¿van a pagar juntos?
are you all paying together?

sí, el servicio (de camareros) está incluido
yes, service is included

FOOD AND DRINK

Understanding

ahumado	smoked
a la parrilla	grilled *(over charcoal etc)*
a la plancha	grilled *(on a hotplate or griddle)*
a la romana	battered and deep fried
aliñado	dressed
asado en horno de leña	roasted in a wood-fired oven
asado	roasted
braseado	braised
cocido	boiled
curado	cured
dorado	browned
empanado	in breadcrumbs
en lonchas	sliced
en puré	puréed
en su punto	just right, done to a turn; *(steak)* medium
en trozos	in pieces
estofado	stewed
fresco	fresh
frío	cold
frito	fried
fundido	melted
hecho	done, cooked
hervido	boiled
poco hecho	rare
rebozado	battered; dipped in flour and beaten egg
relleno	stuffed, filled
salteado	sautéed

◆ desayunos y meriendas breakfasts and snacks

bollo	roll, bun
churro	fritter *(often eaten dipped in thick chocolate)*
magdalena	small sponge cake

mantequilla	butter
margarina	margarine
mermelada	jam
montado	piece of roast or fried meat, served on a piece of bread
rosquilla	type of doughnut
tostada	slice of toast

◆ **aperitivos, tapas y pinchos** appetizers and savoury snacks

The famous Spanish **tapas** can be either small nibbles served with a drink, or cooked food served on small plates and eaten with a fork. **Pinchos** are tapas consisting of a small piece of bread with some sort of topping, held together by a cocktail stick. If you are hungry and want to have tapas as your main meal, ask for a **ración**, which is a larger portion of one of the tapas. There is an infinite variety of different tapas and every region has its own specialities. They are usually eaten standing at the bar, although you can choose to sit at a table instead.

aceitunas	olives
anchoas	salted anchovies
berberechos	cockles
bonito en escabeche con pimientos	pickled tuna with roast peppers
boquerones en vinagre	(fresh) pickled anchovies
boquerones fritos	(fresh) fried anchovies
calamares fritos	fried squid
caracoles	snails
champiñones a la plancha	grilled mushrooms
chopitos fritos	fried cuttlefish
chorizo	spicy pork sausage
criadillas	bull's testicles
croquetas	croquettes

empanada gallega	Galician pasty *(usually contains tuna or cod)*
empanadillas	pasties
ensaladilla rusa	Russian salad
gambas con gabardina	prawns in batter
gambas a la plancha	grilled prawns
gambas cocidas	boiled prawns
jamón de pata negra	high-quality cured ham, from a specific breed of pig
jamón ibérico	high-quality cured ham, from a specific breed of pig
jamón serrano	cured ham
lacón	foreleg of pork, usually boiled or dried and salted
langostinos cocidos	boiled prawns
lomo embuchado	sausage made from loin of pork, which is spiced, dried and salted
mejillones al vapor	steamed mussels
mejillones en salsa	mussels in sauce
mollejas	sweetbreads
morcilla	blood sausage
patatas alioli	potatoes with garlic mayonnaise
patatas bravas	diced, fried potatoes with hot tomato sauce and mayonnaise
patatas fritas	chips, crisps
pepinillos	gherkins
pescadito frito	fried whitebait
pimientos de Padrón	small green peppers *(some are very hot)*
pincho moruno	kebab
pulpo a la gallega	boiled octopus dusted with red pepper
salchichón	type of large, spicy, salami-like sausage
tortilla (de patatas)	potato omelette
tortilla paisana	vegetable omelette

A traditional Spanish lunch consists of a starter (**primer plato**), a main course (**segundo plato**) and a dessert (**postre**). Some dishes which were traditionally starters, such as **paella**, are now often eaten as a meal in themselves (**plato único**) accompanied by a salad, or with a light soup or apéritif to start. The evening meal is usually lighter than lunch, and frequently consists of a sandwich or some tapas. On feast days or special occasions, however, a large dinner resembling the lunch described above is normally served.

◆ primeros platos first courses

acelgas	Swiss chard
ajo blanco	cold soup made with garlic, almonds and bread
alcachofas	artichokes
alubias blancas	haricot beans
alubias rojas	red kidney beans
berenjenas rebozadas	fried aubergines
calabacines rellenos	stuffed courgettes
caldo gallego	Galician broth
consomé	consommé
crema de calabacín	cream of courgette soup
ensalada de lechuga, tomate y cebolla	lettuce, tomato and onion salad
ensalada de pimientos rojos	red pepper salad
ensalada mixta	mixed salad
espaguetis	spaghetti
gazpacho	cold soup, usually made with tomatoes, peppers and garlic, etc
guisantes con jamón	peas sautéed with ham
huevos fritos	fried eggs
huevos rellenos	stuffed eggs *(usually stuffed with tuna)*
judías	beans
judías verdes	runner beans
lentejas	lentils
macarrones	macaroni

menestra de verduras	mixed vegetables
paella	paella
pimientos del piquillo	small, slightly hot red peppers
revuelto de ajetes/de setas/de gambas	scrambled eggs with garlic shoots/mushrooms/prawns
sopa de cocido	soup made with broth, chickpeas and vegetables
sopa de pescado	fish soup
tortilla de gambas/ jamón/espárragos	prawn/ham/asparagus omelette
tortilla francesa	plain omelette

◆ pescados fish dishes

atún encebollado	tuna with onion
bacalao al ajoarriero	flaked salt cod with tomato, peppers, onion and garlic
bacalao a la vizcaína	= **bacalao con tomate**
bacalao al pil-pil	cod in a spicy garlic and olive oil sauce
bacalao con tomate	cod with tomato sauce
bacalao rebozado	cod in batter
besugo a la espalda	baked red sea-bream *(split open down the back)*
bonito con tomate	tuna in tomato sauce
boquerones	fresh anchovies
calamares a la plancha	grilled squid
calamares en su tinta	squid in their ink
chipirones a la plancha	grilled baby squid
chipirones en su tinta	baby squid in their ink
cogote de merluza	baked hake *(the part of the fish just behind the head)*
gallo	John Dory; megrim *(a type of flat fish)*
lenguado a la plancha	grilled sole
lubina a la sal	sea bass baked in salt
lubina al horno	baked sea bass
merluza en salsa verde	hake in green sauce
merluza rebozada	hake in batter
pez espada	swordfish

sardinas	sardines
trucha con jamón	trout fried with ham
ventresca de bonito	belly of tuna

◆ aves y caza poultry and game

codorniz escabechada	pickled quail
codorniz estofada	braised quail
conejo al ajillo	rabbit with garlic
jabalí	wild boar
pato	duck
pechuga empanada	breast of chicken in breadcrumbs
perdiz escabechada	pickled partridge
perdiz estofada	braised partridge
pichón	pigeon
pollo al ajillo	chicken with garlic
pollo asado	roast chicken
pollo en pepitoria	chicken stew with almonds, hard-boiled eggs, white wine and saffron

◆ carnes meat dishes

albóndigas	meatballs
carne estofada	meat stew
cordero asado	roast lamb
chuleta de cerdo	pork chop
chuleta de ternera	veal chop
chuletillas de cordero	lamb chops
chuletillas de lechazo	suckling lamb chops
chuletón de buey	T-bone steak
entrecot	entrecôte steak
escalope	escalope of veal
filete de cerdo	pork fillet
filete de ternera	fillet of veal
lechazo asado	roast suckling lamb
rabo de buey	oxtail
solomillo	sirloin steak
ternera en su jugo	veal cooked in its own juices

◆ postres y dulces desserts and sweets

arroz con leche	rice pudding
brazo gitano	type of sponge roll filled with cream
buñuelos	fritters
compota de manzana	stewed apple
crema catalana	type of crème brûlée
dulce de membrillo	quince jelly
flan	crème caramel
leche frita	squares of thick custard, dipped in egg, fried and served dusted with sugar and cinnamon
macedonia de frutas	fruit salad
mantecado	shortcake biscuit
manzana asada	baked apple
melocotón en almíbar	peaches in syrup
milhoja	puff pastry
natillas	custard
queso de Burgos	type of curd cheese
queso manchego	matured ewe's milk cheese from La Mancha
tarta de almendra	almond tart
tarta de Santiago	almond tart, a speciality of Santiago de Compostela
tocino de cielo	rich dessert made with egg yolks and sugar
torrija	type of French toast

GLOSSARY OF FOOD AND DRINK

aceite oil
aceite de oliva olive oil
achicoria chicory
ácido tart, sour, acid
agridulce sweet-and-sour
aguacate avocado
ajo garlic
albahaca basil
alcachofa artichoke
alcaparras capers
alioli garlic mayonnaise

almejas clams
almendras almonds
almíbar syrup
alubias beans
alubias negras black beans
alubias rojas red kidney beans
anchoas salted anchovies
angulas elvers
apio celery
arándano blackcurrant
arenque herring

arroz rice
asado roast, baked
asar to roast, to bake
atún tuna
avellana hazelnut
azafrán saffron
azúcar sugar
bacón bacon
bacalao cod
bacalao salado salt cod
barbacoa barbecue
barra bar
barra de pan French loaf, baguette
batido milkshake
bechamel béchamel sauce
berenjena aubergine
berros water cress
besugo red sea-bream
bocadillo sandwich *(made with baguette-style bread)*
boquerones fresh anchovies
brócoli broccoli
brotes de soja soy sprouts
budín pudding
calabacín courgette
calabaza pumpkin
calamar squid
caldo broth
calentar to heat (up)
canela cinnamon
canelones cannelloni
carne meat
carne picada minced meat
castaña chestnut
cazón dogfish
cebolla onion
cebolleta type of large spring onion

centollo spider crab
cerdo pork
cerveza beer
chalote shallot
champiñones mushrooms
chicharro scad, horse mackerel
chocolate chocolate
chorizo highly seasoned pork sausage
cilantro coriander
ciruela plum
ciruela pasa, ciruela seca prune
clara de huevo egg white
clavo clove
cocinar to cook
coco coconut
cochinillo suckling pig
codorniz quail
cogollo lettuce heart, little gem lettuce
col cabbage
coles de Bruselas Brussels sprouts
coliflor cauliflower
comida food
comida basura junk food
comino cumin
conejo rabbit
congelado frozen
congrio conger eel
conservante preservative
conservar to preserve
coñac brandy
copos de avena oatflakes
copos de maíz tostados cornflakes
corazones de alcachofas artichoke hearts
cordero lamb

cortar to cut
costilla rib
crema pastelera confectioner's custard
crudo raw
crujiente crisp, crunchy
cuchara spoon
cucharada spoonful
cucharita, cucharilla teaspoon
cuchillo knife
deshuesado boned
derretido melted
desayuno breakfast
desayunar to have (for) breakfast
diente de ajo clove of garlic
dorada gilthead bream
dulce sweet
dulce de membrillo quince jelly
empanada pasty
empanadilla small pasty
en lata tinned, canned
endibias endives
endulzante sweetener
eneldo dill
entero whole
espaguetis spaghetti
espárragos asparagus
especias spices
espeso thick
espina (fish)bone
espinacas spinach
espuma foam
fécula starch
fideuá type of paella made with noodles rather than rice
filete fillet
freír to fry
fresa strawberry

frigorífico refrigerator
fruta fruit
galleta biscuit, cookie
galleta salada savoury biscuit, cracker
gambas prawns
garbanzos chickpeas
granos de pimienta peppercorns
grasa fat
gratinar to grill, to brown under the grill
guarnición accompaniment (to the main part of a dish)
guindilla hot pepper (sometimes pickled)
guisantes peas
habas broad beans
harina flour
helado ice cream
hervir to boil
hierbabuena mint
hígado liver
higo fig
hinojo fennel
hojaldre puff pastry
horno oven
hueso bone
huevas roe
huevo egg
huevo duro hard-boiled egg
ingredientes ingredients
jabalí wild boar
jamón ham
jamón York boiled ham
jerez sherry
langostinos prawns
lata tin, can
laurel bayleaf

leche milk
leche cuajada curd
lechuga lettuce
lentejas lentils
liebre hare
lima lime
limón lemon
maduro mature, ripe
mahonesa mayonnaise
maíz maize; sweetcorn
manteca lard
mantequilla butter
manzana apple
margarina margarine
mariscos seafood
mayonesa mayonnaise
mejillones mussels
melocotón peach
melón melon
membrillo quince
menta mint
merluza hake
miel honey
migas breadcrumbs
mora blackberry
morcilla blood sausage, type of black pudding
morcón type of large sausage, eaten cold
mostaza mustard
muslo de pollo chicken drumstick
naranja orange
nata cream
nata montada whipped cream
nectarina nectarine
nevera refrigerator
nueces walnuts
nuez moscada nutmeg

orégano oregano
paella paella
pan bread
pan de molde sliced bread
pan integral wholemeal bread
panceta bacon
parrillada grill, barbecue
pasa currant
pasta pasta
pastas biscuits; cakes
pastel cake; gateau
patatas potatoes
patatas fritas chips; crisps
pato duck
pechuga de pollo breast of chicken
pepinillo gherkin
pepino cucumber
perdiz partridge
perejil parsley
perrito caliente hotdog
pescado fish
pez espada swordfish
picante hot, spicy
pimentón paprika
pimienta pepper
pimiento rojo red pepper
pimiento verde green pepper
piña pineapple
piñones pine nuts
plátano banana
plato dish; course; plate
plato combinado meal served together on one plate, instead of as separate dishes
pollo chicken
postre dessert
pulpo octopus

puerros leeks
queso cheese
rábano radish
rabo de buey oxtail
rape monkfish, anglerfish
receta recipe
refresco soft drink
remolacha beetroot
riñones kidneys
rodaballo turbot
romero rosemary
sabor taste, flavour
sal salt
salado salted; salty; savoury
salchicha sausage
salmón salmon
salmonete red mullet
salsa sauce
sardinas sardines
sartén frying pan
semillas seeds
setas wild mushrooms

sidra cider
sofrito fried tomato, onion and garlic
solomillo sirloin
tallarines tagliarini *(type of pasta)*
tarta de queso cheesecake
tenedor fork
ternera veal
tierno tender
tocino bacon
tomate tomato
tomillo thyme
torrija type of French toast
tortilla (de patatas) potato omelette
tostado slice of toast
trucha trout
vinagre vinegar
vino wine
yema de huevo egg yolk
yemas small sweets made with egg yolks and sugar

Spain is known for its vibrant nightlife. Going out for **el fin de semana** (the weekend) is a ritual in Spain, but even on Thursdays there are plenty of people out and about. On Fridays and Saturdays the streets are almost invariably thronged with people. The Spanish go out late – generally from about 10 or 11pm, often staying out until dawn. In Madrid and Barcelona, you can find plenty of information about what's on in the **Guía del Ocio** (out every Thursday), which covers shows, concerts, nightclubs and so on. You can also consult **Metrópoli**, the **El Mundo** newspaper's Friday supplement, or the **El País** supplement for detailed information on Madrid or Barcelona's lively cultural scene. In other areas see the local paper.

Going to the cinema in Spain is cheaper than in the UK, but note that foreign-language films are almost always dubbed into Spanish. Films that are not dubbed are labelled **versión original subtitulada**, often abbreviated to **V.O. subtitulada**.

Spanish nightclubs are generally open until the small hours (between 3 and 5am) and the minimum age for admittance is 18.

The basics

ballet	ballet *ba-let*
band	grupo *groo-poh*
bar	bar *bah*
cinema	cine *thee-nay*
circus	circo *theer-koh*
classical music	música clásica *moo-see-ka kla-see-ka*
club	discoteca *dees-koh-tay-ka*
concert	concierto *kon-thyair-toh*
dubbed film	película doblada *pe-lee-koo-la dob-lah-da*
festival	festival *fes-tee-bal*
film	película *pe-lee-koo-la*
folk music	música popular *moo-see-ka pop-oo-lah*
group	grupo *groo-poh*
jazz	jazz *yaz*
modern dance	danza moderna *dan-tha mod-air-na*

musical	musical *moo-see-kal*
party	fiesta *fyes-ta*
pop music	música pop *moo-see-ka pop*
rock music	música rock *moo-see-ka rok*
show	espectáculo *es-pek-tak-oo-loh*
subtitled film	película subtitulada *pe-lee-koo-la soob-tee-too-lah-da*
theatre	teatro *tay-at-roh*
ticket	entrada *en-trah-da*
to book	reservar *res-air-bah*
to go out	salir *sa-leer*
to play	(*music*) poner *pon-air*

SUGGESTIONS AND INVITATIONS

Expressing yourself

where can we go?
¿dónde podemos ir?
don-day pod-ay-mos eer

what do you want to do?
¿qué quieres hacer?
kay kyair-es a-thair

shall we go for a drink?
¿vamos a tomar una copa?
bah-mos a toh-mah oo-na koh-pa

what are you doing tonight?
¿qué haces esta noche?
kay a-thes es-ta no-chay

do you have plans?
¿tienes planes?
tyen-es plan-es

would you like to …?
¿te gustaría …?
tay goos-ta-ree-a …

we were thinking of going to …
estábamos pensando en ir a …
es-tah-ba-mos pen-san-doh en eer a …

I can't today, but maybe some other time
hoy no puedo, pero quizás otro día
oy noh pway-doh, peh-roh kee-thas oh-troh dee-a

I'm not sure I can make it
creo que no puedo
kray-oh kay noh pway-doh

I'd love to
me encantaría
may eng-kan-ta-ree-a

ARRANGING TO MEET

Expressing yourself

what time shall we meet?
¿a qué hora quedamos?
a kay aw-ra kay-dah-mos

where shall we meet?
¿dónde quedamos?
don-day kay-dah-mos

would it be possible to meet a bit later?
¿podemos quedar un poco más tarde?
pod-ay-mos kay-dah oon poh-koh mas tah-day

see you tomorrow night
nos vemos mañana
nos bay-mos man-yah-na

I have to meet … at nine
he quedado con … a las nueve
ay kay-dah-doh kon … a las nway-bay

I don't know where it is, but I'll find it on the map
no sé dónde está, pero lo encontraré en el mapa
no say don-day es-ta, peh-roh loh eng-kon-tra-ray en el ma-pa

I'll meet you later, I have to stop by the hotel first
nos vemos luego, tengo que pasar por el hotel primero
nos bay-mos lway-goh, teng-goh kay pa-sah paw el oh-tel pree-mair-oh

I'll call/text you if there's a change of plan
ya te llamo/mando un mensaje si hay cambio de planes
ya tay yah-mo/man-doh oon men-sa-CHay see hay cam-bee-oh day plan-es

are you going to eat first?
¿vas a comer antes?
bas a kom-air an-tes

sorry I'm late
siento llegar tarde
syen-toh yay-gah tah-day

Understanding

¿te parece bien?
is that ok with you?

nos vemos allí
I'll meet you there

podemos quedar fuera
we can meet outside

pasaré a recogerte sobre las ocho
I'll come and pick you up about 8

te voy a dar mi número y puedes llamarme mañana
I'll give you my number and you can call me tomorrow

GOING OUT

Some informal expressions

tomar una copa to have a drink
picar algo to have a bite to eat
pasarlo en grande to have a whale of a time

FILMS, SHOWS AND CONCERTS

Expressing yourself

is there a guide to what's on?
¿hay una guía del ocio?
eye oo-na gee-a del ohth-yoh

I'd like three tickets for ...
quiero tres entradas para ...
kyair-oh tres en-trah-das pa-ra ...

two tickets, please
dos entradas, por favor
dos en-trah-das, paw fa-vaw

it's called ...
se llama ...
say yah-ma ...

I've seen the trailer
he visto el tráiler
ay bees-toh el treye-lair

what time does it start?
¿a qué hora empieza?
a kay aw-ra em-pyay-tha

I'd like to go and see a show
me gustaría ir a ver un espectáculo
may goos-ta-ree-a eer a bair oon es-pek-tak-oo-loh

I'll find out whether there are still tickets available
voy a ver si quedan entradas
boy a bair see kay-dan en-trah-das

how long is it on for?
¿cuánto dura?
kwan-toh doo-ra

do we need to book in advance?
¿hay que reservar con antelación?
eye kay res-air-bah kon an-tay-lath-yohn

are there tickets for another day?
¿hay entradas para otro día?
eye en-trah-das pa-ra oh-troh dee-a

I'd like to go to a bar with some live music
me gustaría ir a un bar con música en vivo
may goos-ta-ree-a eer a oon bah con moo-see-ka en bee-boh

are there any free concerts?	**what sort of music is it?**
¿hay conciertos gratis?	¿qué tipo de música es?
eye kon-thyair-tohs gra-tees	*kay tee-poh day moo-see-ka es*

Understanding

cine de arte y ensayo	arthouse cinema
matiné	matinée
película taquillera	blockbuster
reservas	bookings
taquilla	box office

| **estreno en cines el …** | **es un concierto al aire libre** |
| on general release from … | it's an open-air concert |

ha tenido muy buenas críticas
it's had very good reviews

| **la dan en el Odeón a las ocho** | **la estrenan la semana que viene** |
| it's on at 8pm at the Odeón | it comes out next week |

| **esa sesión está agotada** | **está todo agotado hasta …** |
| that showing's sold out | it's all booked up until … |

no hace falta reservar con antelación
there's no need to book in advance

la obra dura hora y media con el entreacto
the play lasts an hour and a half, including the interval

por favor apaguen sus teléfonos móviles
please turn off your mobile phones

PARTIES AND CLUBS

Expressing yourself

I'm having a leaving party tonight
voy a dar una fiesta de despedida esta noche
boy a dah oo-na fyes-ta day des-pe-dee-da es-ta no-chay

we could go to a club afterwards
podemos ir a una discoteca luego
po-day-mos eer a oo-na dees-koh-tay-ka lway-goh

should I bring something to drink?
¿traigo algo de beber?
treye-goh al-goh de be-bair

do you have to pay to get in?
¿hay que pagar entrada?
eye kay pa-gah en-trah-da

I have to meet someone inside
he quedado con alguien dentro
ay kay-dah-doh kon al-gyen den-troh

will you let me back in when I come back?
¿me dejarás entrar cuando vuelva?
may day-CHa-ras en-trah kwan-doh bwel-ba

do you come here often?
¿vienes mucho por aquí?
byen-es moo-choh paw a-kee

the DJ's really cool
el disk-jockey es genial
el dees-yok-ey es CHen-yal

can I buy you a drink?
¿me dejas que te invite a una copa?
may day-CHas kay tay een-bee-tay a oo-na koh-pa

no thanks, I don't smoke
no gracias, no fumo
noh grath-yas, noh foo-moh

thanks, but I'm with my boyfriend
gracias, pero estoy con mi novio
grath-yas, peh-roh es-toy kon mee nohv-yoh

Understanding

consumisión gratis	free drink
guardarropa	cloakroom
7 euros despúes de las 12	€7 after midnight
verbena	open-air party *(the most famous is on Midsummer's Eve, 23 June)*

hay una fiesta en la casa de Elena
there's a party at Elena's place

¿quieres bailar?
do you want to dance?

eres muy guapo/a
you're very handsome/beautiful

¿tienes fuego?
have you got a light?

¿tienes un cigarro?
have you got a cigarette?

¿quedamos para otro día?
can we see each other again?

¿puedo acompañarte a casa?
can I see you home?

TOURISM AND SIGHTSEEING

Museums in Spain are generally open every day (although some are closed on Mondays), but close early on Sundays and bank holidays (at 2 or 2.30 pm). Most museums, as well as many monuments and churches, charge an admission fee. Student discounts are available and some museums have free admission on the first Sunday or Thursday of the month. Opening hours may change according to the season.

The basics

ancient	antiguo *an-**tee**-gwoh*
antique *(noun)*	antigüedad *an-tee-gway-**dad***
area	zona *__thoh__-na*
castle	castillo *kas-**teel**-yoh*
cathedral	catedral *ka-tay-**dral***
century	siglo *__see__-gloh*
church	iglesia *ee-__glay__-sya*
exhibition	exposición *eks-pos-eeth-__yohn__*
gallery	galería *ga-le-__ree__-a*
modern art	arte moderno *ah-tay mo-__dair__-noh*
mosque	mezquita *meth-__kee__-ta*
museum	museo *moo-__say__-oh*
painting	*(art)* pintura *pin-__too__-ra*; *(picture)* cuadro *kwad-roh*
park	parque *__pah__-kay*
ruins	ruinas *roo-__ee__-nas*
sculpture	escultura *es-kool-__too__-ra*
statue	estatua *es-__tat__-wa*
street map	plano *__plah__-noh*
synagogue	sinagoga *see-na-__goh__-ga*
tour guide	guía turistico *__gee__-a too-__rees__-ti-ka*
tourist	turista *too-__rees__-ta*

| tourist information centre | oficina de turismo *o-fee-thee-na day too-rees-moh* |
| town centre | centro (de la ciudad) *then-troh (day la thyoo-dad)* |

Expressing yourself

I'd like some information on …
quisiera información sobre …
kees-yair-a een-faw-math-yohn soh-bray …

can you tell me where the tourist information centre is?
¿puede decirme dónde está la oficina de turismo?
pway-day de-theer-may don-day es-ta la o-fi-thee-na day too-rees-moh

do you have a street map of the town?
¿tiene un plano de la ciudad?
tyen-ay oon plah-noh day la thyoo-dad

I was told there's a castle around here
me han dicho que hay un castillo por aquí
may an dee-choh kay eye oon kas-teel-yoh paw a-kee

can you show me where it is on the map?
¿me lo puede señalar en el mapa?
may loh pway-day sen-ya-lah en el ma-pa

how do you get there?	**is it free?**
¿cómo se llega allí?	¿es gratis?
kom-oh say yay-ga al-yee	*es gra-tees*

when was it built?
¿cuándo fue construido?
kwan-don fway kons-troo-ee-doh

Understanding

abierto	open
casco antiguo	old town
cerrado	closed
entrada gratuita	admission free
gótico	Gothic

guerra	war
invasión	invasion
medieval	medieval
renovación	renovation
romano	Roman
trabajos de restauración	restoration work
usted está aquí	you are here *(on a map)*
visita guiada	guided tour

pregunte cuando llegue allí
you'll have to ask when you get there

la proxima visita guiada empieza a las dos
the next guided tour starts at 2 o'clock

MUSEUMS, EXHIBITIONS AND MONUMENTS

Expressing yourself

I've heard there's a ... exhibition on at the moment
he oido que hay una exposición de … ahora
ay o-ee-doh kay eye oo-na eks-pos-eeth-yohn day … a-aw-ra

how much is it to get in?
¿cuánto es la entrada?
kwan-toh es la en-trah-da

is this ticket valid for the exhibition as well?
¿esta entrada también es válida para la exposición?
es-ta en-trah-da tam-byen es bal-ee-da pa-ra la eks-pos-eeth-yohn

are there any discounts for young people?
¿hay descuentos para jóvenes?
eye des-kwen-tohs pa-ra CHoh-ben-es

is it open on Sundays?
¿está abierto los domingos?
es-ta ab-yair-toh los do-meen-gohs

two concessions and one full price, please
por favor, una entrada normal y dos con descuento
paw fa-vaw, oo-na en-trah-da nawr-mal ee dos kon des-kwen-toh

I have a student card
tengo carné de estudiante
teng-goh kah-nay day es-tood-yan-tay

audioguía	audioguide
exposición permanente	permanent exhibition
exposición temporal	temporary exhibition
por aquí	this way
prohibido hacer fotos	no photography
prohibido usar el flash	no flash photography
se ruega no tocar	please do not touch
silencio, por favor	silence, please
taquilla	ticket office

la entrada al museo cuesta ...
admission to the museum costs ...

con esta entrada también puede entrar a la exposición
this ticket also allows you access to the exhibition

¿tienes el carnet de estudiante?
do you have your student card?

GIVING YOUR IMPRESSIONS

it's beautiful
es precioso
es preth-yoh-soh

it was beautiful
era precioso
air-a preth-yoh-soh

it's fantastic
es fantástico
es fan-tas-ti-koh

it was fantastic
era fantástico
air-a fan-tas-ti-koh

I really enjoyed it
me ha gustado mucho
may a goos-tah-doh moo-choh

I didn't like it that much
no me ha gustado mucho
noh may a goos-tah-doh moo-choh

it was a bit boring
era un poco aburrido
air-a oon poh-koh a-bu-rree-doh

I'm not really a fan of modern art
no me interesa mucho el arte moderno
noh may een-tay-ray-sa moo-choh el ah-tay mo-dair-noh

it's expensive for what it is
es caro para lo que es
es kah-roh pa-ra loh kay es

it's very touristy
es muy turístico
es mwee too-rees-ti-koh

it was really crowded
había mucha gente
a-bee-a moo-cha CHen-tay

we didn't go in the end, the queue was too long
al final no entramos, había desmasiada cola
al fee-nal noh en-trah-mos, a-bee-a de-mas-yah-da koh-la

we didn't have time to see everything
no tuvimos tiempo de verlo todo
noh too-bee-mos tyem-poh day bair-loh toh-doh

Understanding

famoso	famous
pintoresco	picturesque
típico	typical
tradicional	traditional

tienes que ir a ver …
you really must go and see …

recomiendo que vayas a …
I recommend going to …

hay una vista preciosa de toda la ciudad
there's a wonderful view over the whole city

se ha vuelto demasiado turístico
it's become a bit too touristy

SPORTS AND GAMES

Those interested in going hiking in Spain will find plenty of information and maps in tourist offices (**oficinas de turismo**). All year long, thousands of pilgrims and walkers take the famous path to Santiago de Compostela (known as the **camino de Santiago**). Cycling is also popular in Spain, while skiing is possible in the Pyrenees and the Sierra Nevada. Many Spaniards are still avid fans of bullfighting. Certain football matches arouse national passion, such as those between rival teams **Real Madrid** and **Barça** (from Barcelona), **Betis** and **Sevilla** (both Seville teams) or **Bilbao** and **Real Sociedad** (both Basque teams). There are also many golf courses, especially in holiday areas, and very good conditions for windsurfing may be found, particularly at Tarifa and in the Canaries.

The basics

ball	balón *ba-lohn*
basketball	baloncesto *ba-lohn-thes-toh*
bike	bicicleta *bee-thee-klay-ta*
board game	juego de mesa *CHway-goh day may-sa*
cards	cartas *kah-tas*
chess	ajedrez *a-CHed-reth*
cross-country skiing	esquí de fondo *es-kee day fon-doh*
cycling	ciclismo *thee-kleez-moh*
downhill skiing	esquí alpino *es-kee al-pee-noh*
football	fútbol *foot-bol*
hiking path	sendero *sen-dair-oh*
match	partido *pah-tee-doh*
mountain biking	ciclismo de montaña *thee-kleez-moh day mon-tan-ya*
pool	(game) billar (americano) *beel-yah (a-mair-ee-kah-noh)*
rugby	rugby *roog-bi*
skiing	esquí *es-kee*
snowboarding	snowboarding *es-noh-bawr-ding*

sport	deporte *day-paw-tay*
surfing	surfing *soor-fing*
swimming	natación *na-tath-yohn*
swimming pool	piscina *pees-thee-na*
table football	futbolín *foot-bol-een*
tennis	tenis *ten-ees*
trip	viaje *bee-a-CHay*
waterskiing	esquí acuático *es-kee a-kwat-ee-koh*
to go hiking	hacer senderismo *a-thair sen-dair-eez-moh*
to have a game of ...	jugar a ... *CHoo-gah a ...*
to play	jugar a *CHoo-gah a*
to ski	esquiar *es-kee-ah*

Expressing yourself

are there ... lessons available?
¿dan clases de ...?
dan klas-es day ...

I'd like to hire ... for an hour
quiero alquilar... por una hora
kyair-oh al-kee-lah ... paw oo-na aw-ra

how much is it per person per hour?
¿cuánto es a la hora por persona?
kwan-toh es a la aw-ra paw pair-soh-na

I'm not very sporty
no se me dan bien los deportes
noh say may dan byen los day-paw-tays

I've done it once or twice, a long time ago
lo hice una o dos veces hace mucho tiempo
loh ee-thay oo-na oh dos beth-ays a-thay moo-choh tyem-poh

I'm exhausted!
¡estoy agotado!
es-toy a-goh-tah-doh

I've never done it before
nunca lo he hecho
nung-ka loh ay e-choh

I'd like to go and watch a football match
me gustaría ir a ver un partido de fútbol
may goos-ta-ree-a eer a bair oon pah-tee-doh day foot-bol

shall we stop for a picnic?
¿paramos a tomar algo?
pa-rah-mos a tom-ah al-goh

we played ...
jugamos a ...
CHoo-gah-mos a ...

Understanding

¿tienes experiencia o eres principiante?
do you have any experience, or are you a complete beginner?

hay una fianza de ...   **alquiler de ...**
there is a deposit of ...   ... for hire

el seguro es obligatorio y cuesta ...
insurance is compulsory and costs ...

HIKING

Expressing yourself

can you go hiking round here?
¿se puede hacer senderismo por aquí?
say pway-day a-thair sen-dair-**eez**-moh paw a-**kee**

can you recommend any good walks in the area?
¿puede recomendarme unas buenas rutas por esta zona?
pway-day re-kom-en-**dah**-may **oo**-nas **bway**-nas **roo**-tas paw es-ta **thoh**-na

I've heard there's a nice walk by the lake
me han dicho que hay un paseo muy bonito por el lago
may an **dee**-choh kay eye oon pa-**say**-oh mwee bon-**ee**-toh paw el **lah**-goh

we're looking for a short walk somewhere round here
queremos dar un pequeño paseo por aquí
kair-**ay**-mos dah oon pe-**kayn**-yoh pa-**say**-oh paw a-**kee**

can I hire hiking boots?
¿alquilan botas de senderismo?
al-**kee**-lan **boh**-tas day sen-dair-**eez**-moh

how long does the hike take?   **where's the start of the path?**
¿cuánto dura la ruta?   ¿dónde empieza el sendero?
kwan-toh **doo**-ra la **roo**-ta   don-day em-**pyay**-tha el sen-**dair**-oh

is it very steep?   **is the path waymarked?**
¿está muy empinado?   ¿está señalizado el sendero?
es-**ta** mwee em-pee-**nah**-doh   es-**ta** sen-ya-lee-**thah**-doh el sen-**dair**-oh

is it a circular path?
¿el sendero da una vuelta completa?
el sen-dair-oh da oo-na bwel-ta com-play-ta

duración media
average duration *(of walk)*

la ruta dura unas tres horas, contando los descansos
it's about three hours' walk, including rest stops

traiga chaqueta impermeable y calzado de senderismo
bring a waterproof jacket and some walking shoes

SKIING AND SNOWBOARDING

Expressing yourself

I'd like to hire skis, sticks and boots
quiero alquilar esquís, bastones y botas
kyair-oh al-kee-lah es-kees, bas-toh-nays ee boh-tas

I'd like to hire a snowboard
quiero alquilar una tabla de snowboarding
kyair-oh al-kee-lah oo-na tab-la day es-noh-bawr-ding

they're too big/small
me quedan grandes/pequeños
may kay-dan gran-days/pe-kayn-yohs

a day pass
un forfait para un día
oon faw-fet pa-ra oon dee-a

I'm a complete beginner
soy principiante total
soy preen-theep-yan-tay toh-tal

Understanding

forfait	lift pass
telearrastre	T-bar, button lift
telesilla	chair lift
telesquí	ski lift

OTHER SPORTS

Expressing yourself

where can we hire bikes?
¿dónde podemos alquilar bicicletas?
don-day pod-ay-mos al-kee-lah bee-thee-klay-tas

does anyone have a football?
¿tiene alguien un balón?
tyen-ay al-gyen oon ba-lohn

are there any cycle paths?
¿hay carriles-bici?
eye ka-RRee-lays bee-thee

which team do you support?
¿de qué equipo eres?
day kay ay-kee-poh ay-res

I support ...
yo soy del ...
yoh soy del ...

is there an open-air swimming pool?
¿hay piscina al aire libre?
eye pees-thee-na al eye-ray lee-bray

I've never been diving before
nunca he hecho buceo
nung-ka ay e-choh boo-thay-oh

I'd like to take beginners' sailing lessons
quiero dar unas clases de vela para principiantes
kyair-oh dah oo-nas klas-ays day bay-la pa-ra preen-theep-yan-tays

I run for half an hour every morning
corro media hora todas las mañanas
koRR-oh med-ya aw-ra toh-das las man-yah-nas

what do I do if the kayak capsizes?
¿qué hago si el kayak se vuelca?
kay ah-goh see el ka-yak say bwel-ka

Understanding

hay una pista de tenis municipal cerca de la estación
there's a public tennis court near the station

la pista de tenis está ocupada
the tennis court's occupied

¿es la primera vez que monta a caballo?
is this the first time you've been horse-riding?

¿sabe nadar?
can you swim?

¿juega al baloncesto?
do you play basketball?

INDOOR GAMES

Expressing yourself

shall we have a game of cards?
¿echamos una partida de cartas?
e-*chah*-mos *oo*-na pah-*tee*-dah day *kah*-tas

does anyone know any good card games?
¿alguien sabe un buen juego de cartas?
al-*gyen* sa-*bay* oon bwen *CHway*-goh day *kah*-tas

is anyone up for a game of Monopoly®?
¿alguien quiere echar una partida de Monopoly®?
al-*gyen* kyair-ay e-*chah* *oo*-na pah-*tee*-da day mo-no-*pohl*-ee

it's your turn
te toca
tay *toh*-ka

Understanding

¿sabes jugar al ajedrez?
do you know how to play chess?

¿tienes una baraja de cartas?
do you have a pack of cards?

Some informal expressions

estoy hecho polvo I'm absolutely knackered
me ha machacado he totally thrashed me

75

SHOPPING

Shops in Spain are generally open Monday to Saturday, from 9am to 1.30 or 2pm and then from 4 or 5pm to 8.30pm. However, some department stores and supermarkets stay open over lunch, and later at night. Hypermarkets and shopping centres are usually open from 10am to 10pm. Cigarettes are much cheaper than in the UK and are sold in tobacconists (**estancos**) or from vending machines in bars. If you pay for purchases by credit or debit card, you will be given the receipt to sign and will always be asked for ID. In some areas, small shops are not open on Saturday afternoons. In holiday areas, opening hours vary according to the season, with many shops also opening on Sundays.

Traditional markets play a key role in Spanish life, despite stiff competition from supermarkets. Most markets are open every day except Sunday, traditionally only in the morning, although some now reopen in the afternoon, especially on Fridays.

Some informal expressions

¡eso es un robo! that's a rip-off!
estoy sin blanca I'm broke
cuesta un ojo de la cara it costs an arm and a leg
es una ganga it's a real bargain
precios rebajados prices slashed

The basics

bakery	panadería *pan-a-dair-ee-a*
butcher's	carnicería *kah-nee-thair-ee-a*
cash desk	caja *ka-CHa*
cheap	barato *ba-rat-oh*
checkout	caja *ka-CHa*
clothes	ropa *roh-pa*

department store	grandes almacenes *gran-days al-ma-then-ays*
expensive	caro *kah-roh*
gram	gramo *grah-moh*
greengrocer's	(shop) verdulería *bair-doo-lair-ee-a*; (sign) frutas y verduras *froo-tas ee bair-doo-ras*
hypermarket	hipermercado *ee-pair-mair-kah-doh*
kilo	kilo *kee-loh*
present	regalo *re-gah-loh*
price	precio *preth-yoh*
receipt	recibo *re-thee-boh*
refund	devolución *day-bol-ooth-yohn*
sales	rebajas *re-ba-CHas*
sales assistant	dependiente *day-pen-dyen-tay*
shop	tienda *tyen-da*
shopping centre	centro comercial *then-troh kom-air-thyal*
souvenir	recuerdo *rek-wair-doh*
supermarket	supermercado *soo-pair-mair-kah-doh*
to buy	comprar *kom-prah*
to cost	costar *kos-tah*
to pay	pagar *pa-gah*
to refund	devolver *day-bol-bair*
to sell	vender *ben-dair*

SHOPPING

Expressing yourself

is there a supermarket near here?
¿hay un supermercado cerca?
eye oon soo-pair-mair-kah-doh thair-ka

where can I buy cigarettes?
¿dónde puedo comprar tabaco?
don-day pway-doh kom-prah ta-bak-oh

I'm looking for …
estoy buscando …
es-toy boos-kan-doh …

I'd like …
quiero …
kyair-oh …

do you sell …?
¿venden …?
ben-den …

do you know where I might find some …?
¿sabe dónde puedo encontrar …?
sab-ay don-day pway-doh eng-kon-trah …

can you order it for me?
¿me lo puede pedir?
may loh pway-day pe-deer

how much is this?
¿cuánto es esto?
kwan-toh es es-toh

I'll take it
me lo quedo
may loh kay-doh

it's eight euros fifty
son ocho euros (con) cincuenta
son o-choh ay-oo-rohs (kon) theeng-kwen-ta

I haven't got much money
no tengo mucho dinero
noh teng-goh moo-choh dee-nair-oh

I haven't got enough money
no tengo suficiente dinero
noh teng-goh soo-feeth-yen-tay dee-nair-oh

that's everything, thanks
eso es todo, gracias
es-oh es toh-doh, grath-yas

can I have a (plastic) bag?
¿me da una bolsa (de plástico)?
may dah oo-na bol-sa (day plas-tee-koh)

I think you've made a mistake with my change
creo que me ha dado mal la vuelta
kray-oh kay may a dah-doh mal la bwel-ta

Understanding

abierto de … a …	open from … to …
cerrado domingos/de 1 a 3 de la tarde	closed Sundays/1pm to 3pm
oferta especial	special offer
rebajas	sales

¿quiere alguna cosa más?
will there be anything else?

¿quiere una bolsa?
would you like a bag?

PAYING

Expressing yourself

how much do I owe you?
¿cuánto le debo?
kwan-toh lay day-boh

where do I pay?
¿dónde se paga?
don-day say pah-ga

could you write it down for me, please?
¿me lo puede escribir, por favor?
may loh pway-day es-kree-beer, paw fa-vaw

can I pay by credit card?
¿puedo pagar con tarjeta de crédito?
pway-doh pa-gah kon tah-CHay-tah day kred-ee-toh

I'm sorry, I haven't got any change
lo siento, no tengo cambio
loh syen-toh, noh teng-goh kam-byoh

can I have a receipt?
¿me da un recibo?
may da oon re-thee-boh

I'll pay in cash
voy a pagar en efectivo
boy a pa-gah en ef-ek-tee-boh

can you give me change for a 50-euro note, please?
¿puede cambiarme un billete de 50 euros?
pway-day kamb-yah-may oon beel-yay-tay day theeng-kwen-ta ay-oo-rohs

Understanding

pague en caja
pay at the cash desk

¿cómo quiere pagar?
how would you like to pay?

¿tiene algún documento de identidad?
have you got any ID?

firme aquí, por favor
could you sign here, please?

¿tiene algo más pequeño?
do you have anything smaller?

FOOD

Expressing yourself

where can I buy food around here?
¿dónde puedo comprar comida por aquí?
don-day pway-doh kom-prah kom-ee-da paw a-kee

is there a market?
¿hay un mercado?
eye oon mair-kah-doh

is there a bakery around here?
¿hay una panadería por aquí?
eye oo-na pan-a-dair-ee-a paw a-kee

I'm looking for the cereals
estoy buscando los cereales
es-toy boos-kan-doh los thair-ray-ah-les

I'd like five slices of ham
quiero cinco lonchas de jamón
kyair-oh theeng-koh lon-chas day CHa-mohn

I'd like some of that goat's cheese
quiero un poco de ese queso de cabra
kyair-oh oon poh-koh day e-say kay-soh day kab-ra

it's for four people
es para cuatro personas
es pa-ra kwat-roh pair-soh-nas

about 300 grams
unos trescientos gramos
oo-nohs tres-thyen-tohs grah-mohs

a kilo of apples, please
un kilo de manzanas
oon kee-loh day man-thah-nas

a bit less/more
un poco menos/más
oon poh-koh may-nohs/mas

can I taste it?
¿puedo probarlo?
pway-doh proh-bah-loh

does it travel well?
¿se conserva bien en el viaje?
say kon-sair-va byen en el bee-a-CHay

Understanding

casero	homemade
orgánico	organic
productos locales	local specialities

consumir preferentemente antes de …
best before …

el café está en el tercer pasillo a la derecha
the coffee's in the third aisle on the right

hay un mercado que abre diariamente hasta la una
there's a market every day until 1pm

**hay una tienda de comestibles en la esquina que abre hasta
tarde**
there's a grocer's just on the corner that's open late

CLOTHES

Expressing yourself

I'm looking for the menswear section
estoy buscando la sección de caballero
es-*toy* boos-*kan*-doh la sek-*thyohn* day ka-bal-*yair*-oh

no thanks, I'm just looking
no gracias, sólo estoy mirando
noh *grath*-yas, *soh*-loh es-*toy* mee-*ran*-doh

can I try it on?
¿puedo probármelo?
pway-doh prob-*ah*-may-loh

do you have it in another colour?
¿lo tiene en otro color?
loh *tyen*-ay en *oh*-troh ko-*law*

I'd like to try the one in the window
me gustaría probarme el del escaparate
may goos-ta-*ree*-a prob-*ah*-may el del es-kap-a-*rat*-ay

I take a size 40 (in shoes)
calzo el 40
kal-thoh el kwa-*ren*-tah

where are the changing rooms?
¿dónde están los probadores?
don-day es-*tan* los prob-a-*daw*-rays

it doesn't fit
no me queda bien
noh may *kay*-da byen

it's too big/small
me queda grande/pequeño
may *kay*-da *gran*-day/pe-*kayn*-yoh

do you have it in a smaller/bigger size?
¿lo tiene en una talla menor/mayor?
loh *tyen*-ay en *oo*-na *tal*-ya men-*aw*/meye-*aw*

do you have them in red?
¿los tiene en rojo?
los tyen-ay en ro-CHoh

yes, that's fine, I'll take them
sí, me están bien, me los quedo
see, may es-tan byen, may los kay-doh

no, I don't like it
no, no me gusta
noh, noh may goos-ta

I'll think about it
me lo voy a pensar
may loh boy a pen-sah

I'd like to return this, it doesn't fit
quisiera devolver esto, no me queda bien
kees-yair-a day-bol-bair es-toh, noh may kay-da byen

this ... has a hole in it, can I get a refund?
este ... tiene un agujero, ¿puede devolverme el dinero?
es-tay ... tyen-eh oon a-goo-CHair-oh, pway-day day-bol-bair-may el dee-nair-oh

Understanding

abierto domingos	open Sunday
no se aceptan devoluciones	no returns
probadores	changing rooms
ropa de caballero	menswear
ropa de señora	ladieswear
ropa infantil	children's clothes
ropa interior	lingerie

hola, ¿qué desea?
hello, can I help you?

sólo lo tenemos en azul o en negro
we only have it in blue or black

no nos queda ninguno en esa talla
we don't have any left in that size

le queda bien
it suits you

puede devolverlo si no le queda bien
you can bring it back if it doesn't fit

SOUVENIRS AND PRESENTS

Expressing yourself

I'm looking for a present to take home
estoy buscando un regalo para llevar a casa
es-*toy* boos-*kan*-doh oon reg-*ah*-loh *pa*-ra yay-*bah* a *ka*-sa

I'd like something that's easy to transport
quiero algo que sea fácil de transportar
kyair-oh *al*-goh kay *say*-a *fath*-eel day trans-paw-*tah*

it's for a little girl of four
es para una niña de cuatro años
es *pa*-ra *oo*-na *neen*-ya day *kwat*-roh *an*-yohs

could you gift-wrap it for me?
¿puede envolvérmelo en papel de regalo?
pway-day em-bol-*bair*-may-loh en pa-*pel* day reg-*ah*-loh

Understanding

fabricado en madera/   made of wood/silver/gold/wool
  plata/oro/lana
hecho a mano   handmade
productos artesanales   traditionally made products

¿cuánto quiere gastar?
how much do you want to spend?

¿es para regalo?
is it for a present?

es típico de la región
it's typical of the region

PHOTOS

Understanding

black and white	blanco y negro *blang-koh ee nay-groh*
camera	cámara *kam-a-ra*
colour	color *kol-aw*
copy	copia *kop-ya*
digital camera	cámara digital *kam-a-ra dee-CHee-tal*
disposable camera	cámara desechable *kam-a-ra des-ech-ah-blay*
exposure	exposición *eks-pos-eeth-yohn*
film	carrete *ka-RRay-tay*
flash	flash *flas*
glossy	con brillo *kon breel-yoh*
matte	mate *ma-tay*
memory card	tarjeta de memoria *tah-CHay-ta day mem-aw-rya*
negative	negativo *nay-ga-tee-boh*
passport photo	foto carné *foh-toh kah-nay*
photo booth	fotomatón *foh-toh-ma-tohn*
reprint	copia *kop-ya*
slide	diapositiva *dee-a-pos-ee-tee-va*
to get photos developed	revelar fotos *RRe-ve-lah foh-tohs*
to take a photo/photos	hacer una foto/unas fotos *a-thair oo-na foh-toh/oo-nas foh-tohs*

Expressing yourself

could you take a photo of us, please?
¿nos puede hacer una foto, for favor?
nos pway-day a-thair oo-na foh-toh, paw fa-vaw

you just have to press this button
sólo tiene que apretar este botón
soh-loh tyen-ay kay a-pret-ah es-tay bo-tohn

I'd like a 200 ASA colour film
quiero un carrete a color de doscientos ASA
kyair-oh oon ka-RRay-tay a kol-aw day dos-thyen-tohs a-sa

do you have black and white films?
¿tiene carretes en blanco y negro?
tyen-ay ka-RRay-tays en blang-koh ee nay-groh

how much is it to develop a film of 36 photos?
¿cuánto cuesta revelar un carrete de treinta y seis fotos?
kwan-toh kwes-ta RRe-ve-lah oon ka-RRay-tay day trayn-ta ee says foh-tohs

I'd like to have this film developed
¿me puede revelar este carrete?
may pway-day RRe-ve-lah es-tay ka-RRay-tay

I'd like extra copies of some of the photos
quiero hacer copias de algunas fotos
kyair-oh a-thair kop-yas day al-goo-nas foh-tohs

three copies of this one and two of this one
tres copias de ésta y dos de ésta
trays kop-yas day es-ta ee dos day es-ta

can I print my digital photos here?
¿imprimen fotos digitales?
im-pree-men foh-tohs dee-CHee-tah-les

can you put these photos on a CD for me?
¿me puede grabar estas fotos en un CD?
may pway-day gra-bah es-tas foh-tohs en oon thay-day

I've come to pick up my photos
vengo a recoger mis fotos
beng-go a RRe-ko-CHair mees foh-tohs

I've got a problem with my camera
mi cámara tiene un problema
mee kam-a-ra tyen-ay oon prob-lay-ma

I don't know what it is
no sé lo que es
noh say loh kay es

the flash doesn't work
el flash no funciona
el flas noh foon-thyoh-na

Understanding

formato normal standard format
fotos en CD photos on CD
revelado de fotos en una hora photos developed in one hour
servicio rápido express service

quizás se le ha acabado la pila
maybe the battery's dead

tenemos una máquina para imprimir fotos digitales
we have a machine for printing digital photos

¿a qué nombre?
what's the name, please?

¿para cuándo las quiere?
when do you want them for?

las podemos revelar en un hora
we can develop them in an hour

las fotos estarán listas el jueves por la tarde
your photos will be ready on Thursday afternoon

PHOTOS

BANKS

Most banks in Spain are open from 8am to 2pm, Monday to Friday, and some are also open on Saturday morning. You can withdraw money from the numerous cashpoints (**cajeros automáticos**) with an international credit card, which can also be used in most shops, hotels and restaurants. You will be asked to show ID when paying. Although the euro has been the official currency since 2002, people still sometimes talk in pesetas and peseta equivalents may still be seen on some price tags.

The basics

bank	banco *bang-koh*
bank account	cuenta bancaria *kwen-ta bang-kah-rya*
banknote	billete *beel-yay-tay*
bureau de change	(oficina de) cambio *(o-fee-thee-nah day) kam-byoh*
card	tarjeta *tah-CHay-ta*
cashpoint	cajero (automático) *ka-CHair-oh (ow-toh-mat-ee-koh)*
céntimo	cent *then-tee-moh*
change	cambio *kam-byoh*
cheque	cheque *chay-kay*
coin	moneda *mon-ay-da*
commission	comisión *kom-ees-yohn*
credit card	tarjeta de crédito *tah-CHay-ta day kred-ee-toh*
euro	euro *ay-oo-roh*
PIN (number)	número personal *noo-may-roh pair-sohn-al*
transfer	transferencia *trans-fair-enth-ya*
Travellers Cheques®	cheques de viaje *chay-kays day bee-a-CHay*
withdrawal	reintegro *ray-een-tay-groh*
to change	cambiar *kam-byah*
to transfer	transferir *trans-fair-eer*
to withdraw	sacar *sa-kah*

Expressing yourself

where I can get some money changed?
¿dónde puedo cambiar dinero?
don-day pway-doh kam-byah dee-nair-oh

are banks open on Saturdays?
¿los bancos abren los sábados?
los bang-kohs ab-ren los sab-a-dohs

I'm looking for a cashpoint
estoy buscando un cajero
es-toy boos-kan-doh oon ka-CHair-oh

I'd like to change £100
quiero cambiar cien libras
kyair-oh kam-byah thyen lee-bras

what commission do you charge?
¿qué comisión tienen?
kay kom-ees-yohn tyen-en

I'd like to transfer some money
quiero transferir dinero
kyair-oh trans-fair-eer dee-nair-oh

I'd like to report the loss of my credit card
quiero denunciar la pérdida de mi tarjeta de crédito
kyair-oh den-oon-thyah la pair-dee-da day mee tah-CHay-ta day kred-ee-toh

the cashpoint has swallowed my card
el cajero se ha tragado mi tarjeta
el ka-CHair-oh say a tra-gah-doh mee tah-CHay-ta

Understanding

idioma
select language required

teclee su número personal
please enter your PIN number

reintegro sin justificante
withdrawal without receipt

fuera de servicio
out of service

introduzca su tarjeta
please insert your card

reintegro con justificante
withdrawal with receipt

elija importe
please select the amount you require

POST OFFICES

ⓘ

Spanish postboxes are yellow. Stamps can be bought at post offices (**Correos**), which are open from 8.30am to 8.30pm Monday to Friday and from 9.00am to 2.00pm on Saturday, or at tobacconists (**estancos**), which, like most shops, close for a long lunch break. The price of a stamp depends on the destination, so it's best to ask for a stamp (**sello**) for wherever you are sending your mail.

The basics

airmail	por avión *paw ab-yohn*
envelope	sobre *soh-bray*
letter	carta *kah-ta*
mail	correo *ko-RRay-oh*
parcel	paquete *pa-kay-tay*
post	correo *ko-RRay-oh*
postbox	buzón *boo-thohn*
postcard	postal *poh-stal*
postcode	código postal *koh-dee-goh poh-stal*
post office	(Oficina de) Correos *(of-ee-thee-na day)* *ko-RRay-ohs*
stamp	sello *sel-yoh*
to post	mandar por correo *man-dah paw ko-RRay-oh*
to receive	recibir *re-thee-beer*
to send	enviar *en-byah*
to write	escribir *es-kree-beer*

Expressing yourself

is there a post office around here?
¿hay una Oficina de Correos por aquí?
eye oo-na of-ee-thee-na day ko-RRay-ohs paw a-kee

is there a postbox near here?
¿hay un buzón por aquí cerca?
eye oon boo-thohn paw a-kee thair-ka

is the post office open on Saturdays?
¿Correos abre los sábados?
ko-RRay-os ab-ray los sab-a-dohs

what time does the post office close?
¿a qué hora cierra Correos?
a kay aw-ra thee-eRR-a ko-RRay-ohs

how much is a stamp for the UK ?
¿cuánto cuesta un sello para el Reino Unido?
kwan-toh kwes-ta oon sel-yoh pa-ra el RRay-noh oo-nee-doh

I'd like … stamps for the UK, please
por favor, quiero … sellos para el Reino Unido
paw fa-vaw, kyair-oh … sel-yohs pa-ra el RRay-noh oo-nee-doh

where can I buy envelopes?
¿dónde venden sobres?
don-day ben-den soh-brays

do you sell stamps?
¿vende sellos?
ben-day sel-yohs

I'd like to send this parcel to London
quiero enviar este paquete a Londres
kyair-oh en-byah es-tay pa-kay-tay a lon-dres

how long will it take to arrive?
¿cuánto tardará en llegar?
kwan-toh tah-da-ra en yay-gah

my address is …
mi dirección es …
mee dee-rek-thyohn es …

is there any post for me?
teng-goh ko-RRay-oh
¿tengo correo?

In Spain, the house number is given after the street name. So for example, "23 Antonio Machado Street" would be written as "calle Antonio Machado, 23", or abbreviated to "c/ Antonio Machado, 23". For flats, the floor and door numbers are often given in the address. So **4º** refers to the floor (**cuarto piso**), and **2ª** to the door (**segunda puerta**). But be aware that floor numbering can be misleading as many buildings have a **planta baja** (ground floor) and an **entresuelo** (mezzanine), abbreviated to **entlo**. This means that the **primer piso** may actually be the second floor! The top floor is sometimes not numbered, but is called the **ático**. A full address might read as follows: **c/ Antonio Machado, 23 4º 2ª, 22000 Huesca**.

Understanding

destinatario	recipient
frágil	fragile
recogida mañanas	first collection
recogida tardes	afternoon collection
remitente	sender
última recogida	last collection
¿cuál es su dirección?	**tardará entre tres y cinco días**
what's your address?	it'll take between three and five days

Understanding Spanish addresses

Some common abbreviations are **c/** for calle, **Pza.** for plaza, **Avda** for avenida, **Pº** for paseo, **Ctra** for carretera and **s/n** for sin número (when the address doesn't have a house number).

INTERNET CAFÉS AND E-MAIL

www

There are more and more Internet cafés in Spain, and it is becoming increasingly common to exchange e-mail addresses with people. The Spanish use the international (QWERTY) keyboard.

The "at" sign is called an **arroba** (*a-RRoh-ba*), a dot is a **punto** (*poon-toh*) and a dash is a **guión** (*gee-ohn*). **Todo junto** (*toh-doh CHoon-toh*) means that a part of the address is all one word. So for example, the address mariajimenez@wanadoo.es would be given as "maria jimenez (todo junto) arroba wanadoo punto es" (*ma-ree-a CHee-may-neth toh-doh CHoon-toh a-RRoh-ba wa-na-doo poon-toh ay-say*).

The basics

"at" sign	arroba *a-RRoh-ba*
e-mail	email *ee-mayl*
e-mail address	(dirección de) email (*dee-RRek-thyohn day*) *ee-mayl*
Internet café	cibercafé *thee-bair-ka-fay*
key	tecla *tek-la*
keyboard	teclado *tek-lah-doh*
mouse	ratón *ra-tohn*
to copy	copiar *cop-yah*
to cut	cortar *kaw-tah*
to delete	eliminar *e-lee-mee-nah*
to download	bajarse *ba-CHah-say*
to e-mail someone	mandar un email a alguien *man-dah oon ee-mayl a al-gyen*
to key	teclear *tek-lay-ah*
to paste	pegar *peg-ah*
to receive	recibir *reth-ee-beer*
to save	guardar *gwah-dah*
to send an e-mail	enviar un email *en-byah oon ee-mayl*

Expressing yourself

Is there an Internet café near here?
hay un cibercafé por aquí?
ye oon thee-bair-ka-**fay** paw a-**kee**

do you have an e-mail address?
tienes correo electrónico?
tyen-es ko-**RRay**-oh el-ek-tron-ee-koh

how do I get online?
cómo entro en Internet?
kom-oh **en**-troh en een-tair-**net**

I'd just like to check my e-mails
sólo quiero comprobar mi correo
soh-loh **kyair**-oh kom-pro-**bah** mee ko-**RRay**-oh

I'd like to open an e-mail account
quisiera abrir una cuenta de correo electrónico
kees-**yair**-ah a-**breer** oo-na **kwen**-ta day ko-**RRay**-oh el-ek-**tron**-ee-koh

would you mind helping me, I'm not sure what to do
puede ayudarme? no sé bien lo que hay que hacer
pway-day a-yoo-**dah**-may. noh say byen loh kay eye kay a-**thair**

I can't find the "at" sign on this keyboard
no sé dónde está la arroba en este teclado
no say **don**-day es-**ta** la a-**RRoh**-ba en **es**-tay tek-**lah**-doh

there's something wrong with the computer, it's frozen
algo le pasa al ordenador, se ha bloqueado
al-goh lay **pa**-sa al aw-day-na-**daw**, say ah blok-ay-**ah**-doh

how much will it be for half an hour?
cuánto cuesta la media hora?
kwan-toh **kwes**-ta la **med**-ya **aw**-ra

can I make a phone call via the Internet?
se puede llamar por teléfono a través de Internet?
say **pway**-day yam-**ah** paw te-**lay**-fon-oh a tra-**bays** day een-tair-**net**

it's not working
no funciona
noh foon-**thyoh**-na

when do I pay?
cuándo se paga?
kwan-doh say **pah**-ga

Understanding

bandeja de entrada   inbox
bandeja de salida   outbox

escriba su palabra clave para conectarse
just enter this password to log on

pregunte si no sabe lo que hay que hacer
just ask if you're not sure what to do

tiene que esperar unos veinte minutos
you'll have to wait 20 minutes or so

TELEPHONE

Public telephones are often open, which can make things difficult if you have to contend with traffic noise, roadworks and so on. Note that if you make a call from a public phone, you cannot be called back as they do not have numbers. Many phones now take phonecards (**tarjetas telefónicas**), although most still accept coins (**monedas**).

Phonecards are sold in some tobacconists (**estancos**) and newspaper kiosks (**quioscos**). Prepaid cards (**tarjetas prepago**) are becoming increasingly common, and have the advantage that you can use them from private phones as well as phonebooths. They also tend to offer better value on international calls.

Spanish phone numbers have nine digits. The numbers for directory enquiries (**información**) are as follows: 11822 (Spanish numbers) and 11825 (international numbers). Emergency services may be reached by dialling 112 and for medical emergencies the number is 061.

To call the UK from Spain, you need to dial 00 44 followed by the phone number (remember to drop the first 0 of the area code). To call the US, dial 00 1 followed by the area code and phone number. To call Spain from abroad, dial 00 34 followed by the full 9-digit number.

The basics

answering machine	contestador (automático) kon-tes-ta-*daw* (*ow-toh-mat*-ee-koh)
call	llamada yam-*ah*-da
cellphone	móvil *mob*-eel
directory enquiries	información telefónica een-faw-math-*yohn* te-lay-*fon*-ee-ka
hello	(when answering) ¿dígame? *dee*-ga-may; (when calling) hola *oh*-la
international call	llamada internacional yam-*ah*-da een-tair-nath-yoh-*nal*
local call	llamada local yam-*ah*-da loh-*kal*
message	mensaje men-*sa*-CHay

95

mobile	móvil *mob-eel*
national call	llamada nacional *yam-ah-da nath-yoh-nal*
phone	teléfono *te-lay-fon-oh*
phone book	guía telefónica *gee-a te-lay-fon-ee-ka*
phone box	cabina telefónica *ka-bee-na te-lay-fon-ee-ka*
phone call	llamada telefónica *yam-ah-da te-lay-fon-ee-ka*
phone number	número de teléfono *noo-mair-oh day te-lay-fon-oh*
phonecard	tarjeta telefónica *tah-CHay-ta te-lay-fon-ee-ka*
ringtone	señal de llamada *sen-yal day yam-ah-da*
telephone	teléfono *te-lay-fon-oh*
top-up card	tarjeta prepago *tah-CHay-ta pray-pah-goh*
Yellow Pages®	Páginas Amarillas® *pa-CHee-nas a-ma-reel-yas*
to call	llamar *yam-ah*
to call someone	llamar a alguien *yam-ah a al-gyen*
to phone	telfonear *te-lay-fon-ay-ah*

Expressing yourself

where can I buy a phonecard?
¿dónde puedo comprar una tarjeta telefónica?
don-day pway-doh kom-prah oo-na tah-CHay-ta te-lay-fon-ee-ka

a ...-euro top-up card, please
una tarjeta prepago de ... euros, por favor
oo-na tah-CHay-ta pray-pah-goh day ... ay-oo-rohs, paw fa-vaw

I'd like to make a reverse-charge call
quisiera hacer una llamada a cobro revertido
kees-yair-a a-thair oo-na yam-ah-da a kob-roh RRe-bair-tee-doh

is there a phone box near here, please?
perdone, ¿hay una cabina por aquí cerca?
pair-doh-nay, eye oo-na ka-bee-na paw a-kee thair-ka

can I plug my phone in here to recharge it?
¿puedo recargar mi teléfono en este enchufe?
pway-doh RRe-kah-gah mee te-lay-fo-noh en es-tay en-choo-fay

do you have a mobile number?
¿tienes número de móvil?
tyen-es noo-mair-oh day mob-eel

where can I contact you?
¿dónde puedo contactarte?
don-day pway-doh kon-tak-tah-tay

did you get my message?
¿recibiste mi mensaje?
RReth-ee-bee-stay mee men-sa-CHay

el número marcado no existe
the number you have dialled has not been recognized

pulse (la tecla) asterisco/almohadilla
please press the star/hash key

MAKING A CALL

Expressing yourself

hello, this is David Brown (speaking)
hola, soy David Brown
oh-la, soy day-vid brown

hello, could I speak to ..., please?
hola, ¿se puede poner ... por favor?
oh-la, say pway-day pon-air ... paw fa-vaw

do you speak English?
¿hablas inglés?
ab-las eeng-glays

hello, is that María?
hola, ¿eres María?
oh-la, ay-res ma-ree-a

could you speak more slowly, please?
¿puede hablar más despacio, por favor?
pway-day ab-lah mas des-path-yo, paw fa-vaw

I can't hear you, could you speak up, please?
no le oigo, ¿puede hablar más alto, por favor?
noh lay oy-goh, pway-day ab-lah mas al-toh, paw fa-vaw

could you tell him/her I called?
¿puede decirle que le he llamado?
pway-day deth-eer-lay kay lay ay yam-ah-doh

could you ask him/her to call me back?
¿puede decirle que me llame?
pway-day deth-eer-lay kay may yam-ay

I'll call back later
llamaré más tarde
yam-a-ray mas tah-day

thank you, goodbye
gracias, adiós
grath-yas, ad-yohs

my name is … and my number is …
soy … y mi número es el …
soy … ee mee noo-mair-oh es el …

do you know when he/she might be available?
¿sabe cuándo podré hablar con él/ella?
sab-ay kwan-doh pod-ray ab-lah kon el/el-ya

Understanding

se ha equivocado de número
you've got the wrong number

¿de parte de quién?
who's calling?

espere
hold on

no está en este momento
he's/she's not here at the moment

¿quiere dejar un recado?
do you want to leave a message?

le diré que le llame
I'll ask him/her to call you back

le diré que ha llamado
I'll tell him/her you called

ya se lo/la paso
I'll just hand you over to him/her

PROBLEMS

Expressing yourself

I don't know the code
no sé el prefijo
noh say el pre-fee-CHoh

it's engaged
está ocupado
es-ta o-koo-pah-doh

there's no reply	**I couldn't get through to him**
no contesta	no pude hablar con él
*noh kon-**tes**-ta*	*noh **poo**-day ab-**lah** kon el*

I don't have much credit left on my phone
apenas me queda saldo
*a-**pay**-nas may **kay**-da **sal**-doh*

we're about to get cut off	**the reception's really bad**
se va a cortar	se oye muy mal
*say ba a kaw-**tah***	*say **oy**-ay mwee mal*

I can't get a signal
no tengo cobertura
*noh **teng**-goh kob-air-**too**-ra*

Understanding

| **te oigo muy mal** | **se me ha cortado** |
| I can hardly hear you | I got cut off |

Common abbreviations

Tel. (trabajo) = work (number)
Tel. (casa) = home (number)
Tel. Mov. = mobile (number)

Some informal expressions

dar un telefonazo to make a call
colgarle el teléfono a alguien to hang up on somebody

HEALTH	

If you are an EU national, pick up an E111 form from the Post Office before you go to Spain. This ensures that the cost of any medical treatment you may need will be refunded to you when you return home, on production of a receipt.

You can visit a health centre (**Centro de Salud**) or, in an emergency, call 061 or go straight to a hospital's **urgencias** (accident and emergency department).

Prescription drugs can only be obtained from pharmacies (**farmacias**). These are usually open from 9am to 1.30pm and from 4pm to 8pm. A sign on the door shows the address of the nearest duty pharmacist (**farmacia de guardia**). In larger towns there are often 24-hour pharmacies.

The basics

allergy	alergia *al-air-CHya*
ambulance	ambulancia *am-boo-lanth-ya*
aspirin	aspirina *as-pee-ree-na*
blood	sangre *sang-gray*
broken	roto *roh-toh*
casualty (department)	urgencias *oor-CHenth-yas*
chemist's	farmacia *fah-math-ya*
condom	condón *kon-dohn*
dentist	dentista *den-tee-sta*
diarrhoea	diarrea *dee-a-RRay-a*
doctor	médico *may-dee-koh*
food poisoning	intoxicación alimentaria *een-tok-see-kath-yohn a-lee-men-tah-ree-a*
GP	médico de cabecera *may-dee-koh day ka-bay-thair-a*
gynaecologist	ginecólogo *CHee-nay-kol-o-goh*
hospital	hospital *os-pee-tal*
infection	infección *een-fek-thyohn*

medicine	medicina *me-dee-thee-na*
migraine	migraña *mee-gran-ya*
painkiller	analgésico *an-al-CHes-ee-koh*
period	regla *reg-la*
plaster	tirita *tee-ree-ta*
rash	erupción *e-roop-thyohn*
spot	grano *grah-noh*
sunburn	quemadura de sol *kay-ma-doo-ra day sol*
surgical spirit	alcohol *al-ko-ol*
tablet	pastilla *pas-teel-ya*
temperature	fiebre *fyeb-ray*
vaccination	vacuna *ba-koo-na*
x-ray	rayos-X *RReye-ohs ay-kees*
to disinfect	desinfectar *des-een-fek-tah*
to faint	desmayarse *des-meye-ah-say*
to vomit	vomitar *bom-it-ah*

Expressing yourself

does anyone have an aspirin/a tampon/a plaster?
¿tiene alguien una aspirina/un tampon/una tirita?
tyen-ay al-gyen oo-na as-pee-ree-na/oon tam-pohn/oo-na tee-ree-ta

where can I find a doctor?
¿dónde hay un médico?
don-day eye oon may-dee-koh

I need to see a doctor
necesito ver a un médico
neth-e-see-toh bair a oon may-dee-koh

I'd like to make an appointment for today
quisiera pedir cita para hoy
kees-yair-a pe-deer thee-ta pa-ra oy

as soon as possible
lo antes posible
loh an-tes po-see-blay

no, it doesn't matter
no, no importa
noh, noh eem-paw-ta

can you send an ambulance to …
¿puede enviar una ambulancia a …?
pway-day en-byah oo-na am-boo-lan-thya a …

I've broken my glasses
se me han roto las gafas
say may an roh-toh las gaf-as

I've lost a contact lens
he perdido una lentilla
ay pair-dee-doh oo-na len-teel-ya

Understanding

consulta médica   doctor's surgery
receta   prescription
urgencias   accident and emergency department

no hay más citas hasta el jueves
there are no available appointments until Thursday

¿le viene bien el viernes a las dos?
is Friday at 2pm ok?

AT THE DOCTOR'S OR THE HOSPITAL

Expressing yourself

I have an appointment with Dr …
tengo una cita con el doctor …
teng-goh oo-na thee-ta kon el dok-taw …

I feel very weak
me siento muy débil
may syen-toh mwee day-beel

I don't feel very well
no me siento muy bien
noh may syen-toh mwee byen

I don't know what it is
no sé lo que es
noh say loh kay es

I've got a headache
me duele la cabeza
may dway-lay la ka-bay-tha

I've been bitten/stung by …
me ha mordido/picado un …
may a maw-dee-doh/pee-kah-doh oon …

I've got toothache/stomachache
tengo dolor de muelas/dolor de cabeza
teng-goh dol-aw day mway-las/dol-aw day ka-bay-tha

I've got a sore throat
me duele la garganta
may dway-lay la gah-gan-ta

my back hurts
me duele la espalda
may dway-lay la es-pal-da

it hurts
duele
dway-lay

it hurts here
me duele aquí
may dway-lay a-kee

I feel sick
tengo ganas de vomitar
teng-goh gan-as day bom-it-ah

it's got worse
ha empeorado
a em-pay-oh-rah-doh

I've felt like this for three days
me encuentro así desde hace tres días
may eng-kwen-troh a-see dez-day a-thay tres dee-as

it started last night
empezó anoche
em-peth-oh a-no-chay

it's never happened to me before
nunca me ha pasado antes
nung-ka may a pas-ah-doh an-tes

I've got a temperature
tengo fiebre
teng-goh fyeb-ray

I have asthma
tengo asma
teng-goh as-ma

I have a heart condition
estoy enfermo del corazón
es-toy en-fair-moh del ko-ra-thohn

I've been on antibiotics for a week and I'm not getting any better
llevo dos semanas con antibióticos y no mejoro
yay-boh dos se-mah-nas kon an-tee-bee-ot-ee-kohs ee noh may-CHor-oh

it itches
me pica
may pee-ka

I'm on the pill
estoy tomando la píldora
es-toy toh-man-doh la peel-daw-ra

I'm ... months pregnant
estoy embarazada de ... meses
es-toy em-ba-ra-thah-da day .. may-says

I'm allergic to penicillin
soy alérgico a la penicilina
soy a-lair-CHee-koh a la pen-ee-thee-lee-na

I've twisted my ankle
me he torcido el tobillo
may ay taw-thee-doh el tob-eel-yoh

I fell and hurt my back
me he caído y me he hecho daño en la espalda
*may ay ka-**ee**-doh ee may ay e-choh **dan**-yoh en la es-**pal**-da*

I've had a blackout
he tenido un desmayo
*ay te-**nee**-doh oon des-**meye**-oh*

I've lost a filling
se me ha caído un empaste
*say may a ka-**ee**-doh oon em-**pas**-tay*

is it serious?
¿es grave?
*es **grah**-vay*

is it contagious?
¿es contagioso?
*es kon-taCH-**yoh**-soh*

how is he/she?
¿cómo está?
*kom-oh es-**ta***

how much do I owe you?
¿cuánto le debo?
*kwan-toh lay **day**-boh*

can I have a receipt so I can get the money refunded?
¿me da un recibo para que me devuelvan el dinero?
*may da oon re-**thee**-boh **pa**-ra kay may day-**bwel**-ban el dee-**nair**-oh*

Understanding

por favor, pase a la sala de espera
if you'd like to take a seat in the waiting room

¿dónde le duele?
where does it hurt?

respire hondo
take a deep breath

túmbese, por favor
lie down, please

¿le duele si aprieto aquí?
does it hurt when I press here?

¿es usted alérgico a …?
are you allergic to …?

¿se ha vacunado contra …?
have you been vaccinated against …?

¿está tomando otra medicación?
are you taking any other medication?

le voy a hacer una receta
I'm going to write you a prescription

se le pasará en unos días
it should clear up in a few days

se le sanará pronto
it should heal quickly

habrá que operarle
you're going to need an operation

uelva a verme dentro de una semana
come back and see me in a week

AT THE CHEMIST'S

Expressing yourself

I'd like a box of plasters, please
quisiera una caja de tiritas, por favor
kees-*yair*-a oo-na ka-CHa day tee-*ree*-tas, paw fa-*vaw*

Could I have something for a bad cold?
¿me da algo para un resfriado fuerte?
may da *al*-goh *pa*-ra oon res-free-*ah*-doh *fwair*-tay

I need something for a cough
necesito algo para la tos
neth-e-*see*-toh *al*-goh *pa*-ra la tos

I'm allergic to aspirin
soy alérgico a la aspirina
soy a-*lair*-CHee-koh a la as-pee-*ree*-na

I need the morning-after pill
necesito la píldora del día después
neth-e-*see*-toh la *peel*-daw-ra del *dee*-a des-*pwes*

I'd like to try a homeopathic remedy
quisiera probar un remedio homeopático
kees-*yair*-a pro-*bah* oon re-*med*-yoh oh-may-oh-*pat*-ee-koh

I'd like a bottle of solution for soft contact lenses
quisiera un bote de líquido para lentillas blandas
kees-*yair*-a oon *boh*-tay day *lee*-kee-doh *pa*-ra len-*teel*-yas *blan*-das

Understanding

aplicar	to apply
cápsula	capsule
contraindicaciones	contra-indications
crema	cream
en ayunas	on an empty stomach
jarabe	syrup

pastilla	tablet
polvo	powder
pomada	ointment
posibles efectos secundarios	possible side effects
sólo con receta médica	available on prescription only
supositorios	suppositories
tres veces al día antes de las comidas	three times a day before meals

---

Some informal expressions

tener una tos de perro to have a hacking cough
tener un trancazo to have a stinking cold
no estoy muy católico I'm a little off-colour

PROBLEMS AND EMERGENCIES

Be wary of pickpockets and bag snatchers, especially in cities and at popular tourist sites. For lost property, ask for **Objetos perdidos**. In an emergency of any kind, dial 112. If it is specifically a police matter, for example if you lose something or have something stolen, dial 091 for the national police force (**Policía nacional**). Members of the national police force are recognizable by their navy blue uniforms with an arm badge displaying the red and yellow colours of the Spanish flag. Members of the local police force (**Guardia urbana**), also in blue uniforms but with a blue and white badge, deal with more minor matters such as traffic offences, fines and so on; their number is 092. In rural areas, members of the National Guard (**Guardia civil**), who wear dark green uniforms, carry out the duties of the national police force; their number is 062.

The basics

accident	accidente *ak-thee-**den**-tay*
ambulance	ambulancia *am-boo-**lan**-thya*
broken	roto *RRoh-toh*
coastguard	guardacostas *gwah-da-**kos**-tas*
disabled	minusválido *mee-noos-**bal**-ee-doh*
doctor	médico *may-dee-koh*
emergency	urgencia *oor-**CHen**-thya*
fire	fuego *fway-goh*
fire brigade	bomberos *bom-**bair**-ohs*
hospital	hospital *os-pee-**tal***
ill	enfermo *en-**fair**-moh*
injured	herido *e-**ree**-doh*
police	policía *pol-ee-**thee**-a*

Expressing yourself

can you help me?
¿puede ayudarme?
pway-day a-yoo-dah-may

help!
¡socorro!
so-koRR-oh

fire!
¡fuego!
fway-goh

be careful!
¡cuidado!
kwee-dah-doh

it's an emergency!
¡es una urgencia!
es oo-na oor-CHen-thya

there's been an accident
ha habido un accidente
a a-bee-doh oon ak-thee-den-tay

could I borrow your phone, please?
¿puedo usar su teléfono?
pway-doh oo-sah soo te-lay-fon-oh

does anyone here speak English?
¿habla alguien inglés?
ab-la al-gyen eeng-glays

I need to contact the British consulate
tengo que ponerme en contacto con el consulado británico
teng-go kay pon-air-may en kon-tak-toh kon el kon-soo-lah-doh bree-tan-ee-koh

where's the nearest police station?
¿dónde está la comisaría más cercana?
don-day es-ta la kom-ee-sa-ree-a mas thair-kah-na

what do I have to do?
¿qué tengo que hacer?
kay teng-go kay a-thair

my passport/credit card has been stolen
me han robado el pasaporte/la tarjeta de crédito
may an RRoh-bah-doh el pa-sa-paw-tay/la tah-CHay-ta day kred-ee-toh

my bag's been snatched
me han robado el bolso
may han RRoh-bah-doh el bol-soh

I've been attacked
he sufrido una agresión
ay soo-free-doh oo-na ag-res-yohn

I've lost …
he perdido …
ay pair-dee-doh …

my son/daughter is missing
mi hijo/hija se ha perdido
mee ee-CHoh/ee-CHa say a pair-dee-doh

my car's been towed away
la grúa se ha llevado mi coche
la groo-a say a yay-bah-doh mee ko-chay

I've broken down
he tenido una avería
ay ten-ee-doh oo-na a-bair-ee-a

my car's been broken into
me han entrado en el coche
may an en-trah-doh en el ko-chay

there's a man following me
un hombre me está siguiendo
oon om-bray may es-ta see-gyen-doh

is there disabled access?
¿hay acceso para minusválidos?
eye ak-thay-soh pa-ra mee-noos-bal-ee-dohs

can you keep an eye on my things for a minute?
¿puede estar pendiente de mis cosas un minuto?
pway-day es-tah pen-dyen-tay day mees koh-sas oon mee-noo-toh

he's drowning, get help!
se está ahogando, ¡ayuda!
say es-ta a-oh-gan-doh, a-yoo-da

Understanding

averiado	out of order
averías	breakdown service
cuidado con el perro	beware of the dog
objetos perdidos	lost property
salida de emergencia	emergency exit
salvamento de	mountain rescue

POLICE

Expressing yourself

I want to report something stolen
quiero denunciar un robo
kyair-oh day-noon-thyah oon RRoh-boh

I need a document from the police for my insurance company
necesito una copia de la denuncia para mi compañía de seguros
ne-thes-ee-toh oo-na kop-ya day la day-noon-thya pa-ra mee kom-pan-yee a day se-goo-rohs

Understanding

Filling in forms

apellido	surname
nombre	first name
dirección	address
código postal	postcode
país	country
nacionalidad	nationality
fecha de nacimiento	date of birth
lugar de nacimiento	place of birth
edad	age
sexo	sex
duración de la estancia	duration of stay
fecha de llegada/salida	arrival/departure date
profesión	occupation
número de pasaporte	passport number

este producto tiene que pagar impuestos
there's customs duty to pay on this item

¿puede abrir esta maleta, por favor?
would you open this bag, please?

qué falta?
what's missing?

dónde se aloja?
where are you staying?

puede rellenar este impreso, por favor?
would you fill in this form, please?

puede firmar aquí, por favor?
would you sign here, please?

¿cuándo ocurrió?
when did this happen?

¿puede describirlo/la?
can you describe him/it/her?

Some informal expressions

chirona slammer, nick
chorizo thief, crook
¡me han mangado la cartera! my wallet's been pinched!
poli cop

TIME AND DATE

The basics

after	después *des-pways*
already	ya *ya*
always	siempre *syem-pray*
at lunchtime	a mediodía *a med-yoh-dee-a*
at the beginning/end of	al principio/final de *al preen-theep-yoh/fee-nal day*
at the moment	en este momento *en es-tay moh-men-toh*
before	antes *an-tes*
between ... and ...	entre ... y ... *en-tray ... ee ...*
day	día *dee-a*
during	durante *doo-ran-tay*
early	temprano *tem-prah-noh*
evening	noche *no-chay*; (before dark) tarde *tah-day*
for a long time	durante mucho tiempo *doo-ran-tay moo-choh tyem-poh*
from ... to ...	desde ... hasta ... *dez-day ... as-ta ...*
from time to time	de vez en cuando *day beth en kwan-doh*
in a little while	dentro de poco *den-troh day poh-koh*
in the evening	por la noche *paw la no-chay*; (before dark) por la tarde *paw la tah-day*
in the middle of	en mitad de *en mee-tad day*
last	último *ool-tee-moh*
late	tarde *tah-day*
midday	mediodía *med-yoh-dee-a*
midnight	medianoche *med-ya-no-chay*
month	mes *mes*
morning	mañana *man-yah-na*
never	nunca *noong-ka*
next	próximo *prok-see-moh*
night	noche *no-chay*
not yet	todavía no *toh-da-vee-a noh*
now	ahora *a-aw-ra*
occasionally	de vez en cuando *day beth en kwan-doh*
often	a menudo *a men-oo-doh*

rarely	raramente *rah-ra-men-tay*
recently	recientemente *reth-yen-tay-men-tay*
since	desde *dez-day*
sometimes	a veces *a beth-ays*
soon	pronto *pron-toh*
still	todavía *toh-da-bee-a*
straightaway	enseguida *en se-gee-da*
until	hasta *as-ta*
week	semana *sem-ah-na*
weekend	fin de semana *feen day sem-ah-na*
year	año *an-yoh*

Expressing yourself

see you soon!
¡hasta pronto!
as-ta pron-toh

see you later!
¡hasta luego!
as-ta lway-goh

see you on Monday!
¡hasta el lunes!
as-ta el loo-nes

have a good weekend!
¡buen fin de semana!
bwen feen day sem-ah-na

sorry I'm late
siento llegar tarde
syen-toh yay-gah tah-day

I haven't been there yet
no he estado allí todavía
noh ay es-tah-doh al-yee toh-da-bee-a

I've got plenty of time
tengo mucho tiempo
teng-goh moo-choh tyem-poh

I haven't had time to …
no he tenido tiempo de …
noh ay ten-ee-doh tyem-poh day …

I'm in a rush
tengo prisa
teng-goh pree-sa

hurry up!
¡date prisa!
dah-tay pree-sa

just a minute, please
un minuto, por favor
oon min-oo-toh paw fa-vaw

I had a late night
me acosté tarde
may a-kos-tay tah-day a-no-chay

I waited ages
esperé mucho tiempo
es-pair-ay moo-choh tyem-poh

I got up very early
me he levantado temprano
may ay lev-an-tah-doh tem-prah-noh

I have to get up early tomorrow to catch my plane
mañana tengo que levantarme temprano para coger el avión
man-yah-na teng-goh kay leb-an-tah-may tem-prah-noh pa-ra ko-CHair el ab-yohn

we only have 4 days left
sólo nos quedan cuatro días
soh-loh nos kay-dan kwat-roh dee-as

THE DATE

How to write dates

The following examples will show you how dates are written in Spanish:

Tuesday, 5 August 2005	**martes 5 de agosto de 2005**, often shortened to **martes 5/8/2005** ("martes cinco de agosto de dos mil cinco")
2 January 2005	**el dos de enero de dos mil cinco**
in June 2005	**en junio de dos mil cinco**
from 1999 to 2003	**de mil novencientos noventa y nueve a dos mil tres**
in the 21st century	**en el siglo veintiuno**
200 BC	**200 aC** or **200 a. de C.** ("...antes de Cristo")
AD 200	**200 dC** or **200 d. de C.** ("...después de Cristo")

Understanding

... ago	hace ... *a-thay*
in two days' time	dentro de dos días *den-troh day dos dee-as*
last night	anoche *a-no-chay*
the day after tomorrow	pasado mañana *pa-sah-doh man-yah-na*
the day before yesterday	anteayer *an-tay a-yair*
today	hoy *oy*
tomorrow	mañana *man-yah-na*

tomorrow morning/ **afternoon/evening**	manana por la mañana/tarde/noche *man-yah-na paw la man-yah-na/tah-day/no-chay*
yesterday	ayer *a-yair*
yesterday morning/ **afternoon/evening**	ayer por la mañana/tarde/noche *a-yair paw la man-yah-na/tah-day/no-chay*

Expressing yourself

I was born in 1975
nací en 1975
na-thee en meel no-bay-thyen-tos set-en-ta ee theeng-koh

I came here a few years ago
vine aquí hace unos años
bee-nay a-kee a-thay oo-nos an-yohs

I spent a month in Spain last summer
pasé un mes en España el verano pasado
pa-say oon mes en es-pan-ya el bair-ah-no pa-sah-doh

I was here last year at the same time
el año pasado estuve aquí en la misma época
el an-yo pa-sah-doh es-too-bay a-kee en la meez-ma ay-poh-ka

what's the date today?
¿qué fecha es hoy?
kay fe-cha es oy

what day is it today?
¿qué día es hoy?
kay dee-a es oy

it's the 1st of May
es uno de mayo
es oo-no day meye-oh

I'm staying until Sunday
me quedo hasta el domingo
may kay-doh as-ta el dom-eeng-goh

we're leaving tomorrow
nos vamos mañana
nos bah-mos man-yah-na

I already have plans for Tuesday
ya tengo planes para el martes
ya teng-goh plan-es pa-ra el mah-tes

Understanding

una vez/dos veces	once/twice
tres veces a la hora/ **al día**	three times an hour/a day
todos los días	every day
todos los lunes	every Monday

fue construido a mediados del siglo diecinueve
it was built in the mid-nineteenth century

aquí viene mucha gente en verano
it gets very busy here in the summer

¿cuándo te vas?
when are you leaving?

¿cuánto tiempo te quedas?
how long are you staying?

THE TIME

> **Some informal expressions**
>
> **a las dos en punto** at 2 o'clock on the dot
> **son las ocho pasadas** it's after 8 o'clock

The basics

early	temprano *tem-prah-noh*
half an hour	media hora *med-ya aw-ra*
in the afternoon	de la tarde *day la tah-day*
in the morning	de la mañana *day la man-ya-nah*
late	tarde *tah-day*
midday	mediodía *med-yoh-dee-a*
midnight	medianoche *med-ya-no-chay*
on time	a tiempo *a tyem-poh*
quarter of an hour	cuarto de hora *kwah-toh day aw-ra*
three quarters of an hour	tres cuartos de hora *tres kwah-tohs day aw-ra*

Expressing yourself

what time is it?
¿qué hora es?
kay aw-ra es

it's exactly three o'clock
son las tres en punto
son las tres en poon-toh

excuse me, have you got the time, please?
perdone, ¿tiene hora?
pair-doh-nay, tyen-ay aw-ra

it's nearly one o'clock
es casi la una
es *kas*-ee la *oo*-na

it's ten past one
es la una y diez
es la *oo*-na ee *dyeth*

it's a quarter past one
es la una y cuarto
es la *oo*-na ee *kwah*-toh

it's a quarter to one
es la una menos cuarto
es la *oo*-na *may*-nos *kwah*-toh

it's twenty past twelve
son las doce y veinte
son las *doh*-thay ee *bayn*-tay

it's twenty to twelve
son las doce menos veinte
son las *doh*-thay *may*-nos *bayn*-tay

it's half past one
es la una y media
es la *oo*-na ee *med*-ya

I arrived at about two o'clock
llegué sobre las dos
ye-*gay* soh-*bray* las dos

I set my alarm for nine
puse el despertador para las nueve
poo-say el des-pair-ta-*daw* pa-ra las *nway*-bay

I waited twenty minutes
esperé veinte minutos
es-pair-*ay* *bayn*-tay min-*oo*-tohs

the train was fifteen minutes late
el tren llegó con quince minutos de retraso
el trayn yay-*goh* kon *keen*-thay min-*oo*-tohs day ray-*tras*-oh

I got home an hour ago
llegué a casa hace una hora
ye-*gay* a *ka*-sa a-*thay* *oo*-na *aw*-ra

shall we meet in half an hour?
¿quedamos dentro de media hora?
kay-*dah*-mos *den*-troh day *med*-ya *aw*-ra

I'll be back in a quarter of an hour
vuelvo dentro de un cuarto de hora
bwel-boh *den*-troh day oon *kwah*-toh day *aw*-ra

there's a one-hour time difference between … and …
hay una hora de diferencia entre … y …
eye *oo*-na *aw*-ra day dif-air-*en*-thya *en*-tray … ee …

Understanding

sale a la horas y a las medias
departs on the hour and the half-hour

abierto de 10:00 a 16:00
open from 10am to 4pm

abre a las diez de la mañana
it opens at ten in the morning

la dan todas las tardes tardes a las siete
it's on every evening at seven

dura una hora y media más o menos
it lasts around an hour and a half

NUMBERS

0 cero *thair-oh*	**20** veinte *bayn-tay*
1 uno *oo-noh*	**21** veintiuno *bayn-tee-oo-noh*
2 dos *dos*	**22** veintidós *bayn-tee-dos*
3 tres *tres*	**30** treinta *trayn-ta*
4 cuatro *kwat-roh*	**35** treinta y cinco *trayn-ta-ee-theeng-koh*
5 cinco *theeng-koh*	**40** cuarenta *kwa-ren-ta*
6 seis *seys*	**50** cincuenta *theeng-kwen-ta*
7 siete *syet-ay*	**60** sesenta *ses-en-ta*
8 ocho *o-choh*	**70** setenta *set-en-ta*
9 nueve *nway-bay*	**80** ochenta *o-chen-ta*
10 diez *dyeth*	**90** noventa *nob-en-ta*
11 once *on-thay*	**100** cien *thyen*
12 doce *doh-thay*	**101** ciento uno *thyen-toh oo-noh*
13 trece *treth-ay*	**200** doscientos *dos-thyen-tohs*
14 catorce *ka-taw-thay*	**500** quinientos *keen-yen-tohs*
15 quince *keen-thay*	**1000** mil *meel*
16 dieciséis *dyeth-ee-says*	**2000** dos mil *dos meel*
17 diecisiete *dyeth-ee-syet-ay*	**10,000** diez mil *dyeth meel*
18 dieciocho *dyeth-ee-o-choh*	**1,000,000** un millón *oon meel-yohn*
19 diecinueve *dyeth-ee-nway-bay*	

first primero *pree-mair-oh*
second segundo *seg-oon-doh*
third tercero *tair-thair-oh*
fourth cuarto *kwah-toh*
fifth quinto *keen-toh*
sixth sexto *sek-stoh*
seventh séptimo *sep-tee-moh*
eighth octavo *ok-tah-boh*
ninth noveno *nob-ay-noh*
tenth décimo *deth-ee-moh*
twentieth vigesimo/veinteavo *bee-CHes-ee-moh/bayn-tyah-boh*

20 plus 3 equals 23
veinte más tres son veintitrés
*bayn-tay mas tres son bayn-tee-**tres***

20 minus 3 equals 17
veinte menos tres son diecisiete
*bayn-tay **may**-nos tres son dyeth-ee-**syet**-ay*

20 multiplied by 4 equals 80
veinte multiplicado por cuatro son ochenta
*bayn-tay mool-tee-plee-**kah**-doh paw **kwat**-roh son o-**chen**-ta*

20 divided by 4 equals 5
veinte dividido por cuatro son cinco
*bayn-tay di-bee-**dee**-doh paw **kwat**-roh son **theeng**-koh*

DICTIONARY

ENGLISH-SPANISH

a un m/una f *(see grammar)*
abbey abadía f
able: to be able to poder
about sobre; **to be about to
do something** estar a punto de
hacer algo
above sobre
abroad en el extranjero
accept aceptar
access acceso m **109**
accident accidente m **29**, **108**
accommodation alojamiento m
across *(prep)* a través de; **to go
across the street** cruzar la calle
adaptor adaptador m
address dirección f **90**
admission admisión f
advance: in advance por
adelantado **62**
advice consejo m; **to ask someone's advice** pedir consejo a
alguien
advise aconsejar
aeroplane avión m
after *(prep)* después de; **after
dinner** después de cenar
afternoon tarde f; **in the
afternoon** por la tarde
after-sun (cream) after-sun m
again otra vez

against contra
age edad f
air aire m
air conditioning aire m
acondicionado **37**
airline compañía f aérea
airmail correo m aéreo
airport aeropuerto m
alarm clock despertador m
alcohol alcohol m
alive vivo m/viva f
all todo m/toda f, todos mpl/todas
fpl; **all day** todo el día; **all week**
toda la semana; **all the better**
tanto mejor; **all customers** todos
los clientes; **all the time** todo
el tiempo; **all inclusive** todo
incluido
allergic alérgico m/alérgica f **103**,
105
almost casi
already ya
also también
although aunque
always siempre
ambulance ambulancia f **101**
American *(adj)* americano m/
americana f
American *(n)* americano m/
americana f
among entre
anaesthetic anestesia f
and y

animal animal *m*
ankle tobillo *m*
anniversary aniversario *m*
another otro
answer *(n)* respuesta *f*
answer *(v)* responder
answering machine contestador *m* automático
ant hormiga *f*
antibiotics antibióticos *mpl*
anybody, anyone *(no matter who)* cualquiera; **do you know anyone?** ¿conoces a alguien?; **I don't know anyone** no conozco a nadie
anything *(no matter what)* cualquier cosa; **do you want anything?** ¿quieres algo?; **I don't have anything** no tengo nada
anyway *(despite that)* de todas formas; *(changing subject)* bueno
appendicitis apendicitis *f*
appointment cita *f*; **to make an appointment** pedir una cita; **to have an appointment (with)** tener una cita (con) **102**
April abril *m*
area zona *f*; **in the area** en la zona
arm brazo *m*
around *(prep)* alrededor de; **around here** por aquí
arrange arreglar; **to arrange to meet** quedar
arrival llegada *f*
arrive llegar
art arte *m*
artist artista *mf*
as tan; **as soon as possible** lo antes posible; **as well as** así como
ashtray cenicero *m* **43**

ask preguntar; **to ask a questio**[n] hacer una pregunta
aspirin aspirina *f*
asthma asma *m* **103**
at en; **at the corner** en la esqui[na]
attack *(v)* atacar, agredir **109**
August agosto *m*
autumn otoño *m*
available *(thing)* disponible; *(person)* libre
avenue avenida *f*
away: 10 kilometres away a 1[0] kilómetros

B

baby bebé *m*
baby's bottle biberón *m*
back espalda *f*; **at the back of** detrás de
backpack mochila *f*
bad malo, mal; **it's not bad** no está mal
bag *(plastic)* bolsa *f*; *(handbag)* bolso *m*; *(luggage)* maleta *f*
baggage equipaje *m*
baker's panadería *f*
balcony balcón *m*
bandage venda *f*
bank banco *m* **88**
banknote billete *m*
bar bar *m*
barbecue barbacoa *f*
bath baño *m*; **to have a bath** tomar un baño
bathroom cuarto *m* de baño
bath towel toalla *f* de baño
battery *(for torch, radio)* pila; *(for car)* batería **29**
be ser, estar *(see grammar)*
beach playa *f*

beach umbrella sombrilla *f*

beard barba *f*

beautiful bonito *m*/bonita *f*

because porque; **because of** a causa de

bed cama *f*

bee abeja *f*

before *(prep)* antes de; **before dinner** antes de la cena

before *(adv)* antes; **I've seen him before** lo he visto antes

begin empezar

beginner principiante *mf*

beginning principio *m*; **at the beginning** al principio

behind *(prep)* detrás de; **behind the hotel** detrás del hotel

believe creer

below *(prep)* debajo de

beside al lado de

best mejor; **the best** el mejor

better mejor; **to get better** mejorar; **it's better to …** es mejor …

between entre

bicycle bicicleta *f*

bicycle pump bomba *f* de bicicleta

big grande

bike bicicleta *f*

bill *(in restaurant)* cuenta *f* **47**; *(for electricity)* factura *f*

bin *(for rubbish)* cubo *m*

binoculars gemelos *mpl*, prismáticos *mpl*

birthday cumpleaños *m*

bit pedazo *m*

bite *(n)* *(of dog)* mordedura *f*; *(of insect)* picadura *f*; *(snack)* tapa *f*

bite *(v)* morder; *(insect)* picar **102**

black negro *m*/negra *f*

blackout *(of lights)* apagón *m*; *(fainting)* desmayo *m*

blanket manta *f*

bleed sangrar

bless: bless you! ¡Jesús!

blind *(adj)* ciego *m*/ciega *f*

blister ampolla *f*

blood sangre *f*

blood pressure tensión *f* arterial

blue azul

board *(plank)* tabla *f*; **full board** pensión *f* completa; **half board** media pensión *f*

boarding *(of ship, plane)* embarque *m*

boat barco *m*

body cuerpo *m*

book *(n)* libro *m*; **book of tickets** bono *m*

book *(v)* reservar **23**, **44**, **62**

bookshop librería *f*

boot bota *f*; *(of car)* maletero *m*

borrow pedir prestado

botanical garden jardín *m* botánico

both ambos; **both of us** nosotros dos

bottle botella *f*

bottle opener abrebotellas *m*

bottom fondo *m*; **at the bottom (of)** al fondo (de)

bowl bol *m*, cuenco *m*

boy chico *m*, joven *m*; *(child)* niño *m*

boyfriend novio *m*

bra sujetador *m*

brake *(n)* freno *m*

brake *(v)* frenar

bread pan *m*

break romper; **to break one's leg** romperse una pierna

break down (car) tener una avería **29**, **109**

breakdown avería f

breakdown service servicio m de averías

breakfast desayuno m **36**; **to have breakfast** desayunar

bridge puente m

bring traer

brochure folleto m

broken roto m/rota f

bronchitis bronquitis f

brother hermano m

brown marrón; (hair, eyes) castaño m/castaña f

brush cepillo m

build construir

building edificio m

bump (swelling) chichón m; (lump) abolladura f; (on road) bache m; (blow) golpe m

bumper parachoques m

buoy boya f

burn (n) quemadura f

burn (v) quemar; **to burn oneself** quemarse

burst (v) reventar

bus autobús m **27**

bus route línea f de autobús

bus station estación f de autobuses

bus stop parada f de autobuses

busy ocupado m/ocupada f

but pero

butcher's carnicería f

buy comprar **80**

by por; **by car** en coche

bye! ¡adiós!

C

café cafetería f, café m

call (n) llamada f

call (v) llamar **98**

call back (call again) llamar otra vez; (return call) devolver la llamada

camera cámara f

camper (person) campista mf; (vehicle) caravana f

camping campismo m; **to go camping** ir de camping

camping stove cocina f de cámping

campsite cámping m **40**

can (n) lata f

can (v) (be able) poder; (know how) saber; **I can't open this** no puedo abrir esto; **I can't swim** no sé nadar

cancel cancelar

candle vela f

can opener abrelatas m

car coche m **30**, **39**

caravan caravana f

card tarjeta f

car park aparcamiento m, parking m

carry llevar

case caso m; **in case of doubt** en caso de duda; **just in case** por si acaso

cash dinero m efectivo; **to pay cash** pagar en efectivo

cashpoint cajero m automático **8**

castle castillo m

catch (train etc) coger

cathedral catedral f

CD CD m

cell phone (teléfono m) móvil m

cemetery cementerio m

centimetre centímetro *m*

centre centro *m* **36**

century siglo *m*

chair silla *f*

chairlift telesilla *f*

change *(n)* cambio *m* **79**

change *(v)* cambiar **88**

changing room vestuario *m* **81**

channel canal *m*

chapel capilla *f*

charge *(n)* *(price)* precio *m*; **bank charges** comisión *f*; **free of charge** gratis; **service charge** servicio *m*

charge *(v)* *(for product, service)* cobrar

cheap barato *m*/barata *f*

check comprobar

check in *(at airport)* facturar

check-in *(at airport)* facturación *f* **24**

checkout *(counter)* caja *f*

cheers! *(when drinking)* ¡salud!

chemist's farmacia *f*

cheque cheque *m*

chest pecho *m*

child niño *m*/niña *f*

chilly frío *m*/ fría *f*

chimney chimenea *f*

chin barbilla *f*

church iglesia *f*

cigar puro *m*

cigarette cigarrillo *m*

cigarette paper papel *m* de fumar

cinema cine *m*

circus circo *m*

city ciudad *f*

clean *(adj)* limpio *m*/limpia *f*

clean *(v)* limpiar

cliff acantilado *m*

climate clima *m*

climbing *(sport)* montañismo *m*, alpinismo *m*

cloakroom guardarropía *f*; *(toilet)* aseos *mpl*

close *(adj)* cerca; **close to ...** cerca de ...

close *(v)* cerrar

closed cerrado *m*/cerrada *f*

closing time hora *f* de cierre

clothes ropa *f*

clutch *(of car)* embrague *m*

coach autocar *m*

coast costa *f*

coat abrigo *m*

coathanger perchero *m*

cockroach cucaracha *f*

coffee café *m*

coil *(contraceptive)* espiral *f*

coin moneda *f*

Coke® Coca-cola® *f*

cold *(adj)* frío *m*/fría *f*; **it's cold** *(weather)* hace frío; **I'm cold** tengo frío

cold *(n)* resfriado *m*; **to have a cold** estar resfriado

collection *(of stamps etc)* colección *f*; *(of mail)* recogida *f*

colour color *m*

comb *(n)* peine *m*

come venir

come back volver

come in entrar

come out salir

comfortable cómodo *m*/cómoda *f*

company compañía *f*

compartment compartimento *m*

complain quejarse

complaint queja *f*

comprehensive insurance seguro *m* a todo riesgo **30**

computer ordenador *m*

concert concierto m **63**

concert hall sala f de conciertos

concession descuento m **23, 67**

condom condón m

confirm confirmar **25**

connection conexión f **25**

constipated estreñido m/ estreñida f

consulate consulado m

contact (n) contacto m

contact (v) contactar **97, 108**

contact lenses lentillas fpl

contagious contagioso m/ contagiosa f

contraceptive anticonceptivo m

cook (v) cocinar

cooking cocina f; **to do the cooking** hacer la comida

cool fresco m/fresca f

corkscrew sacacorchos m

correct (adj) correcto m/correcta f

cost costar; **how much does it cost?** ¿cuánto cuesta?

cotton algodón m

cotton bud bastoncillo m (de algodón)

cotton wool algodón m (hidrófilo)

cough (n) tos f; **to have a cough** tener tos

cough (v) toser

count contar

country (nation) país m; (countryside) campo m

countryside campo m

course: of course! ¡por supuesto!

cover (n) (on bed) manta f

cover (v) cubrir

credit card tarjeta f de crédito **34, 47, 79**

cross (n) cruz f

cross (v) cruzar

cruise crucero m

cry llorar

cup taza f

currency moneda f

customs aduana f

cut cortar; **to cut oneself** cortarse

cycle path carril-bici m **74**

D

damaged dañado m/dañada f; (clothes) estropeado m/ estropeada

damp húmedo m/húmeda f

dance (n) baile m

dance (v) bailar

dangerous peligroso m/peligrosa

dark oscuro m/oscura f; **dark blue** azul oscuro

date (n) fecha f; **out of date** (invalid) caducado m/caducada f

date from remontarse a

date of birth fecha f de nacimiento

daughter hija f

day día m; **the day after tomorrow** pasado mañana; **the day before yesterday** anteayer

dead muerto m/muerta f

deaf sordo m/sorda f

dear (beloved) querido m/querida (expensive) caro m/cara f

debit card tarjeta f de débito

December diciembre m

declare declarar

deep profundo m/profunda f

degree (temperature) grado m

delay retraso m

delayed retrasado m/retrasada f

deli delicatessen m

dentist dentista mf

deodorant desodorante *m*

department departamento *m*

department store grandes almacenes *mpl*

departure salida *f*

depend depender; **that depends (on)** depende (de)

deposit fianza *f*

dessert postre *m* **45**

develop revelar; **I got the film developed** me revelaron el carrete

diabetes diabetes *f*

diabetic diabético *m*/diabética *f*

dialling code prefijo *m*

diarrhoea diarrea *f*; **to have diarrhoea** tener diarrea

die morir

diesel diesel *m*

diet dieta *f*; **to be on a diet** estar a dieta

different (from) diferente (de)

difficult difícil

digital camera cámara *f* digital

dinner cena *f*; **to have dinner** cenar

direct *(adj)* directo *m*/directa *f*

direction dirección *f*; **to have a good sense of direction** tener buen sentido de la orientación

directory guía *f* telefónica

directory enquiries información *f* telefónica

dirty *(adj)* sucio *m*/sucia *f*

disabled minusválido *m*/minusválida *f* **109**

disaster desastre *m*

disco discoteca *f*

discount descuento *m* **67**; **to give someone a discount** hacerle a alguien un descuento

discount fare precio *m* reducido, tarifa *f* reducida

dish plato *m*; **dish of the day** plato del día

dishes platos *mpl*; **to do the dishes** lavar los platos

dish towel paño *m* de cocina

dishwasher lavavajillas *m*

disinfect desinfectar

disposable desechable

disturb molestar; **do not disturb** no molestar

dive *(into water)* tirarse al agua; *(underwater)* bucear

diving *(underwater)* buceo *m*; **to go diving** bucear

do hacer; **do you have a light?** ¿tienes fuego?

doctor médico *m*/médica *f* **101**

door puerta *f*

door code clave *f* de entrada

downstairs abajo

draught beer cerveza *f* de barril

dress *(n)* vestido *m*

dress *(v)* vestir; **to get dressed** vestirse

dressing *(bandage)* vendaje *m*; *(for salad)* aliño *m*

drink *(n)* bebida *f*; **to go for a drink** ir a tomar una copa **43**; **to have a drink** tomar una copa

drink *(v)* beber **64**

drinking water agua *f* potable

drive: to go for a drive dar una vuelta en coche

drive *(v)* conducir

driving licence carné *m* de conducir

drops gotas *fpl*

drown ahogarse

drugs *(medicine)* medicamentos *mpl*; *(narcotics)* drogas *fpl*
drunk *(adj)* borracho *m*/borracha *f*
dry *(adj)* seco *m*/seca *f*
dry *(v)* secar
dry cleaner's limpieza *f* en seco
duck *(n)* pato *m*
during durante; **during the week** durante la semana
dustbin cubo *m* de la basura
duty chemist's farmacia *f* de guardia

E

each cada; **each one** cada uno
ear oreja *f*
early temprano *m*/temprana *f*
earplugs tapones *mpl* para los oídos
earrings pendientes *mpl*
earth tierra *f*
east este *m*; **in the east** en el este; **(to the) east of** (al) este de
Easter Semana *f* Santa, Pascua *f*
easy fácil
eat comer **43**
economy class clase *f* turista
Elastoplast® tirita *f*
electric eléctrico *m*/eléctrica *f*
electric shaver máquina *f* de afeitar
electricity electricidad *f*
electricity meter contador *m* de la luz
e-mail *(n)* email *m*, correo *m* electrónico **93**
e-mail: to e-mail someone mandar un email a alguien
e-mail address (dirección *f* de)

email *m*/correo *m* electrónico **18**, **93**
embassy embajada *f*
emergency urgencia *f*, emergenc *f* **108**; **in an emergency** en cas de emergencia
emergency exit salida *f* de emergencia
empty vacío *m*/vacía *f*
end fin *m*, final *m*; **at the end of** al final de; **at the end of the street** al final de la calle
engaged ocupado *m*/ocupada *f*
engine motor *m*
England Inglaterra *f*
English *(adj)* inglés *m*/inglesa *f*
English *(n)* *(language)* inglés *m*
enjoy disfrutar; **enjoy your meal!** ¡que aproveche!; **to enjoy oneself** divertirse
enough bastante, suficiente; **that's enough** es suficiente
entrance entrada *f*
envelope sobre *m*
epileptic epiléptico *m*/epiléptica *f*
equipment equipo *m*
espresso café *m* solo, espresso *m*
euro euro *m*
Eurocheque eurocheque *m*
Europe Europa *f*
European *(adj)* europeo *m*/europea *f*
European Union Unión *f* Europea
evening noche *f*; *(before dark)* tarde *f*; **in the evening** por la noche/tarde
every cada; **every day** todos los días

everybody, everyone todo el mundo

everywhere en todos sitios, por todas partes

except excepto

exceptional excepcional

excess baggage exceso m de equipaje

exchange (n) cambio m

exchange rate tipo m de cambio

excuse (n) disculpa f

excuse (v) perdonar; **excuse me** perdona

exhausted agotado m/agotada f

exhaust pipe tubo m de escape

exhibition exposición f **67**

exit salida f

expensive caro m/cara f

expiry date fecha f de caducidad

express (adj) (train) expreso m/expresa f; (letter) urgente

expresso café m solo, espresso m

extra (additional charge) suplemento m

eye ojo m

---

face cara f

facecloth toalla f de cara, manopla

fact hecho m; **in fact** en realidad

faint (v) desmayarse

fair (n) feria f

fall (v) caerse; **to fall asleep** dormirse; **to fall ill** ponerse malo

family familia f

fan (hand-held) abanico m; (electric) ventilador m; (of band) fan mf; (of football team) hincha mf

far lejos; **far from** lejos de

fare precio m

fast rápido m/rápida f

fast-food restaurant restaurante m de cómida rápida

fat gordo m/gorda f

father padre m

favour favor m; **to do someone a favour** hacerle a alguien un favor

favourite favorito m/favorita f

fax fax m

February febrero m

fed up harto m/harta f; **to be fed up (with)** estar harto (de)

feel sentir; **to feel good/bad** sentirse bien/mal

feeling (emotional) sentimiento m; (physical) sensación f

ferry ferry m

festival (party) fiesta f; (cinema, theatre) festival m

fetch ir a buscar; **to go and fetch something/someone** ir a buscar algo/a alguien

fever fiebre f; **to have a fever** tener fiebre

few pocos

fiancé prometido m

fiancée prometida f

fight (n) lucha f

fill llenar

fill in, fill out (form) rellenar

fill up rellenar; **to fill up with petrol** llenar de gasolina

filling (in tooth) empaste m

film (for camera) carrete m **84**, **85**; (movie) película f

finally finalmente

find encontrar
fine (adj) bien; **I'm fine** estoy bien
fine (n) multa f
finger dedo m
finish terminar, acabar
fire fuego m
fire brigade bomberos mpl
fireworks fuegos mpl artificiales
first primero; **first of all** en primer lugar
first class primera clase f
first floor primera planta f
first name nombre m (de pila)
fish (n) pescado m
fishmonger's, fish shop pescadería f
fitting room probador m
fizzy con gas
flash (n) flash m
flask frasco m
flat (adj) llano m/llana f; **flat tyre** rueda desinflada
flat (n) piso m, apartamento m
flavour sabor m
flaw defecto m
flight vuelo m
flip-flops chanclas fpl
floor suelo m; **on the floor** en el suelo
flu gripe f
fly (n) mosca f
fly (v) volar
food comida f
food poisoning intoxicación f alimentaria
foot pie m
for por, para; **for an hour** durante una hora
forbidden prohibido m/prohibida f
forecast (n) pronóstico m
forehead frente f

foreign extranjero m/extranjera f
foreigner extranjero m/extranjer·
forest bosque m
fork tenedor m
forward (adv) hacia adelante
four-star petrol gasolina f súper
fracture (n) fractura f
fragile frágil
France Francia f
free (at no cost) gratis; (at liberty) libr·
freezer congelador m
French (adj) francés m/francesa f
French (n) (language) francés m
Friday viernes m
fridge frigorífico m
fried frito m/frita f
friend amigo m/amiga f
from de, desde; **from ... to ...** de ... a ...
front parte f delantera; **in front ·** delante de
fry freír
frying pan sartén f
full lleno m/llena f; **full of** lleno de
full board pensión f completa
full fare, full price precio m completo
funfair parque m de atracciones
fuse fusible m

G

gallery galería f
game juego m; (match) partido m
garage garaje m
garden jardín m
gas gas m
gas cylinder bombona f de butano
gastric flu afección f gastrointestinal vírica

ate puerta f
auze gasa f
ay gay
earbox caja f de cambios
eneral general
ents' (toilet) servicio m de
caballeros
German (adj) alemán m/alemana f
German (n) (person) alemán
m/alemana f; (language) alemán m
Germany Alemania f
et (bus, train) coger
et off (bus, train) bajarse de
et up levantarse
ift wrap papel m de regalo
irl chica f, joven f; (child) niña f
irlfriend novia f
ive dar
ive back devolver
lass (material) cristal m;
(container) vaso m; **a glass of
water/of wine** un vaso de agua/
de vino
lasses gafas fpl
luten-free sin gluten
o ir; **to go to Madrid/to Spain**
ir a Madrid/a España; **we're
going home tomorrow** nos
vamos a casa mañana
o away irse
o in entrar
o out salir
o out with salir con
olf golf m
olf course campo m de golf
ood bueno m/buena f; **good
morning** buenos días; **good
afternoon** buenas tardes; **good
evening** buenas noches
oodbye adiós
oodnight buenas noches mpl

goods productos mpl
GP médico m/médica f de
cabecera
grams gramos mpl
grass hierba f; (lawn) césped m
great (excellent) estupendo m/
estupenda f
Great Britain Gran Bretaña f
Greece Grecia f
Greek (adj) griego m/griega f
Greek (n) (person) griego m/griega
f; (language) griego m
green verde
greengrocer's verdulería f
grey gris
ground suelo m; **on the ground**
en el suelo; **football ground**
campo de fútbol
ground floor planta f baja
grow crecer
guarantee garantía f
guest huésped mf
guest house pensión f
guide (person) guía mf; (book) guía
f **62**
guidebook guía f
guided tour visita f guiada
guy tío m
gynaecologist ginecólogo m/
ginecóloga f

H

hair pelo m
hairdresser peluquero m/
peluquera f
hairdrier secador m de pelo
half medio m/media f; **half a
litre/kilo** medio litro/kilo; **half an
hour** media hora f
half-board media pensión f

half-pint media pinta f
hand mano f
handbag bolso m
handbrake freno m de mano
handicapped minusválido m/
  minusválida f
handkerchief pañuelo m
hand luggage equipaje m de
  mano
hand-made hecho m/hecha f a
  mano
hangover resaca f; **to have a**
  hangover tener resaca
happen pasar, ocurrir
happy feliz
hard duro m/dura f
hashish hachís m
hat sombrero m
hate odiar
have tener
have to tener que; **I have to go**
  tengo que irme
hay fever alergia f al polen
he él
head cabeza f
headache dolor m de cabeza; **to**
  have a headache tener dolor
  de cabeza
headlight faro m
health salud f
hear oír
heart corazón m
heart attack ataque m al corazón
heat calor m
heating calefacción f
heavy pesado m/pesada f
hello hola
helmet casco m
help (n) ayuda f; **to call for help**
  pedir ayuda; **help!** ¡socorro!
help (v) ayudar **108**

her su; **her car** su coche; **I**
  gave it to her se lo di a ella; **I**
  talked to her hablé con ella (se
  grammar)
here aquí; **here is/are** aquí
  está/están
hers suyo, suya; **it's not my car,**
  it's hers no es mi coche, es el
  suyo (see grammar)
herself ella misma
hi! ¡hola!
high alto m/alta f
high blood pressure
  hipertensión f
high tide marea f alta
hiking senderismo m; **to go**
  hiking hacer senderismo **72**
hill colina f
hill-walking senderismo m; **to g**
  hill-walking hacer senderismo
him a él; **I gave it to him** se lo d
  a él; **I talked to him** hablé con é
  (see grammar)
himself él mismo
hip cadera f
hire (n) alquiler m
hire (v) alquilar **30**, **73**, **74**
his su; **his car** su coche; **it's not**
  mine, it's his no es mío, es suyo
  (see grammar)
hitchhike hacer autoestop
hitchhiking autoestop m
hold sostener
hold on! (on the phone) ¡espere!
holiday(s) vacaciones fpl; **on**
  holiday de vacaciones **16**
holiday camp campamento m
Holland Holanda f
home casa f; **at home** en casa; **t**
  go home irse a casa
homosexual homosexual

honest honesto m/honesta f
honeymoon luna f de miel, viaje m de novios
horse caballo m
hospital hospital m
hot caliente; **it's hot** hace calor; **hot drink** bebida caliente
hot chocolate chocolate m caliente
hotel hotel m
hotplate placa f de cocina
hour hora f; **an hour and a half** una hora y media
house casa f
housework tareas fpl domésticas; **to do the housework** hacer las tareas domésticas
how cómo; **how are you?** ¿cómo estás?
hungry hambriento m/hambrienta f; **to be hungry** tener hambre
hurry (n) prisa f; **to be in a hurry** tener prisa
hurry (up) darse prisa
hurt doler; **it hurts** me duele; **my foot hurts** me duele el pie
husband marido m

I

yo; **I'm English** soy inglés; **I'm 22 (years old)** tengo 22 años
ice hielo m
ice cube cubito m de hielo
identity card carné m de identidad
identity papers documentos mpl de identidad
if si
ill enfermo m/enferma f

illness enfermedad f
important importante
in en; **in England/2007/Spanish** en Inglaterra/2007/español; **in the 19th century** en el siglo diecinueve; **in an hour** dentro de una hora
included incluido m/incluida f
independent independiente
indicator (in car) intermitente m
infection infección f
information información f **66**
injection inyección f
injured herido m/herida f
insect insecto m
insecticide insecticida m
inside dentro
insomnia insomnio m
instant coffee café m instantáneo
instead en cambio; **instead of** en vez de
insurance seguro m
intend to … tener la intención de …
international internacional
international money order giro m postal internacional
Internet internet f
Internet café cibercafé m **93**
invite invitar
Ireland Irlanda f
Irish irlandés m/irlandesa f
iron (n) plancha f
iron (v) planchar
island isla f
it ello; **it's beautiful** es precioso; **it's warm** hace calor
Italian (adj) italiano m/italiana f
Italian (n) (person) italiano m/italiana f; (language) italiano m

Italy Italia *f*
itchy que pica; **it's itchy** pica
item artículo *m*

J

jacket chaqueta *f*
January enero *m*
jetlag jetlag *m*
jeweller's joyería *f*
jewellery joyería *f*
job trabajo *m*
jogging footing *m*
journey viaje *m*
jug jarra *f*
juice *(of fruit)* zumo *m*; *(of meat)* jugo *m*
July julio *m*
jumper jersey *m*
June junio *m*
just justo; **just before** justo antes; **just a little** sólo un poco; **just one** sólo uno; **I've just arrived** acabo de llegar; **just in case** por si acaso

K

kayak kayak *m*
keep mantener
key llave *f* **29**, **36**, **39**
kidney riñón *m*
kill matar
kilometre kilómetro *m*
kind *(sort)* tipo *m*; **what kind of …?** ¿qué tipo de …?
kitchen cocina *f*
knee rodilla *f*
knife cuchillo *m*
knock down *(with car)* atropellar

know *(person)* conocer; *(fact)* saber; **I know her** la conozco; **I don't know** no sé

L

ladies' (toilet) servicio *m* de señoras
lake lago *m*
lamp lámpara *f*
landmark lugar *m* muy conocido
landscape paisaje *m*
language lengua *f*, idioma *m*
laptop ordenador *m* portátil
last *(adj)* *(final)* final; *(past)* pasado *m*/pasada *f*; **last year** el año pasado
last *(v)* durar
late tarde **61**
late-night opening *(on sign)* abrimos hasta tarde
latte café *m* con leche
laugh *(v)* reírse
launderette lavandería *f*
lawyer abogado *m*/abogada *f*
leaflet folleto *m*
leak *(in roof, ceiling)* gotera *f*; *(of gas)* escape *m*; *(hole)* agujero *m*
learn aprender
least: the least el menos; **at least** al menos
leave *(go out)* salir; *(go away)* irse
left izquierda *f*; **to the left (of)** a la izquierda (de)
left-luggage (office) consigna *f*
leg *(of person)* pierna *f*; *(of animal, chair)* pata *f*
lend prestar
lens *(of glasses)* cristal *m*; *(of camera)* lente *f*

enses *(contacts)* lentes *fpl* de contacto

ess menos

et *(allow)* dejar, permitir; *(flat, house)* alquilar

etter carta *f*

etterbox buzón *m*

ibrary biblioteca *f*

ife vida *f*

ift *(elevator)* ascensor *m*; **he gave me a lift home** me llevó a casa

ight *(adj)* claro *m*/clara *f*; **light blue** azul claro

ight *(n)* luz *f*; *(lamp)* lámpara *f*; *(traffic light)* semáforo *m*; *(headlight)* faro *m*; **do you have a light?** ¿tienes fuego?

ight *(v)* *(cigarette)* encender

ight bulb bombilla *f*

ighter mechero *m*

ighthouse faro *m*

like *(adv)* como

like *(v)* gustar; **I'd like …** me gustaría … **8, 18, 80**

ine línea *f* **27**

ip labio *m*

listen escuchar

listings magazine guía *f* del ocio

itre litro *m*

little *(adj)* *(small)* pequeño *m*/pequeña *f*; *(not much)* poco *m*/poca *f*

ittle *(adv)* poco

live *(v)* vivir

liver hígado *m*

iving room sala *f* de estar

ocal time hora *f* local

ock *(v)* cerrar con llave

ong largo *m*/larga *f*; **a long time** mucho tiempo; **how long?** ¿cuánto tiempo?

look *(v)* mirar; **you look tired** tienes aspecto cansado

look after cuidar

look at mirar

look for buscar **77**

look like parecerse a

lorry camión *m*

lose perder **109**; **to get lost** perderse; **to be lost** estar perdido **12**

lot mucho *m*/mucha *f*; **a lot of people** mucha gente

loud alto *m*/alta *f*

low bajo *m*/baja *f*

low blood pressure tensión *f* baja

low-fat bajo *m*/baja *f* en grasa

low tide marea *f* baja

luck suerte *f*

lucky afortunado *m*/afortunada *f*; **to be lucky** tener suerte

luggage equipaje *m* **25**

lukewarm tibio *m*/tibia *f*

lunch comida *f*, almuerzo *m*; **to have lunch** comer, almorzar

lung pulmón *m*

Luxembourg Luxemburgo *m*

luxury *(adj)* lujoso *m*/lujosa *f*

luxury *(n)* lujo *m*

M

magazine revista *f*

maiden name nombre *m* de soltera

mail correo *m*

main principal

main course plato *m* principal

make hacer

man hombre *m*

manage dirigir; **to manage to do something** conseguir hacer algo

manager manager *mf*

many muchos, muchas; **how many?** ¿cuántos?; **how many times?** ¿cuántas veces?

map mapa *m* **12**, **26**, **61**, **66**

March marzo *m*

marina puerto *m* deportivo

market mercado *m*

married casado *m*/casada *f*

mass *(in church)* misa *f*

match *(for fire)* cerilla *f*; *(game)* partido *m*

material *(of clothes)* tejido *m*

matter importar: **it doesn't matter** no importa

mattress colchón *m*

May mayo *m*

maybe quizás

me me; **she looked at me** me miró; **me too** yo también *(see grammar)*

meal comida *f*

mean querer decir; **what does … mean?** ¿qué quiere decir …?; **what does it mean?** ¿qué significa?

medicine medicina *f*

medium *(size)* mediano *m*/mediana *f*; *(meat)* en su punto, medio *m*/media *f*

meet encontrar **61**

meeting reunión *f*

member miembro *m*, socio *m*/socia *f*

menu menú *m*

message mensaje *m* **97**

meter *(for gas, electricity)* contador *m*

metre *(measure)* metro *m*

microwave *(n)* microondas *m*

midday mediodía *m*

middle medio *m*; **in the middle (of)** en medio (de)

midnight medianoche *f*

might poder; **it might rain** puede ser que llueva

mill molino *m*

mind importar; **I don't mind** no me importa

mine *(belonging to me)* mío *m*/mía *f* *(see grammar)*

mineral water agua *f* mineral

minister *(in church)* pastor *m*/pastora *f*

minute minuto *m*; **at the last minute** en el último minuto

mirror espejo *m*

Miss Señorita *f*

miss *(train etc)* perder **25**, **27**; **we missed the ferry** perdimos el ferry; **there are two … missing** faltan dos …; **I miss you** te echo de menos

mistake error *m*; **to make a mistake** cometer un error

mobile (phone) *(teléfono m)* móvil *m* **96**

modern moderno *m*/moderna *f*

moisturizer crema *f* hidratante

moment momento *m*; **at the moment** en este momento

monastery monasterio *m*

Monday lunes *m*

money dinero *m* **78**

month mes *m*

monument monumento *m*

mood humor *m*; **to be in a good/bad mood** estar de buen/mal humor

moon luna *f*

moped ciclomotor *m*

more más; **more than** más que; **much more, a lot more** mucho más; **there's no more …** ya no queda …

morning mañana *f*

morning-after pill píldora *f* del día después **105**

mosque mezquita *f*

mosquito mosquito *m*

most más; **the most** el más; **the most expensive one** el más caro; **most people** la mayoría de la gente

mother madre *f*

motorbike moto(cicleta) *f*

motorway autopista *f*

mountain montaña *f*

mountain bike bicicleta *f* de montaña

mountain hut refugio *m* de montaña

mouse *(animal, for computer)* ratón *m*

mouth boca *f*

movie película *f*

Mr Señor *m*

Mrs Señora *f*

much mucho *m*/mucha *f*; **how much?** ¿cuánto?; **how much is it?, how much does it cost?** ¿cuánto es?, ¿cuánto cuesta?

muscle músculo *m*

museum museo *m*

music música *f* **62**

must deber; **it must be 5 o' clock** deben ser las cinco; **I must go** tengo que irme

my mi *(see grammar)*

myself yo mismo *m*/yo misma *f*

N

nail *(of finger)* uña *f*; *(metal)* clavo *m*

naked desnudo *m*/desnuda *f*

name nombre *m*; **my name is …** me llamo … **14**

nap siesta *f*; **to have a nap** echar una siesta

napkin servilleta *f*

nappy pañal *m*

national holiday fiesta *f* nacional

nature naturaleza *f*

near cerca; **near the beach** cerca de la playa; **the nearest …** el … más cercano

necessary necesario *m*/necesaria *f*

neck cuello *m*

need *(v)* necesitar

neighbour vecino *m*/vecina *f*

neither ni; **neither do I** (ni) yo tampoco; **neither … nor …** ni … ni …

nervous nervioso *m*/nerviosa *f*

Netherlands los Países Bajos *mpl*

never nunca

new nuevo *m*/nueva *f*

news noticias *fpl*

newsagent *(shop)* quiosco *m* de prensa

newspaper periódico *m*

newsstand quiosco *m* de prensa

New Year Año *m* Nuevo

next *(in time)* siguiente; *(in place)* de al lado

nice *(good-looking)* guapo *m*/guapa *f*; *(kind)* simpático *m*/simpática *f*

night noche *f* **35**

nightclub discoteca *f*

nightdress camisón *m*

no no; **no, thank you** no, gracias; **no idea** ni idea

nobody nadie

noise ruido *m*; **to make a noise** hacer ruido

noisy ruidoso *m*/ruidosa *f*

non-drinking water agua *f* no potable

none ninguno *m*/ninguna *f*

non-smoker no fumador *m*/no fumadora *f*

noon mediodía *m*

north norte *m*; **in the north** en el norte; **(to the) north of** (al) norte de

nose nariz *f*

not no; **not yet** aún no; **not at all** *(you're welcome)* de nada

note nota *f*

notebook cuaderno *m*

nothing nada

novel novela *f*

November noviembre *m*

now ahora

nowadays hoy en día

nowhere en ningún sitio

number número *m*

nurse enfermero *m*/enfermera *f*

O

obvious obvio *m*/obvia *f*

ocean océano *m*

o'clock en punto; **three o'clock** las tres en punto

October octubre *m*

of de

offer *(n)* oferta *f*

offer *(v)* ofrecer

often a menudo

oil aceite *m*

ointment pomada *f*

OK vale; **are you OK?** ¿estás bien

old antiguo *m*/antigua *f*; **how old are you?** ¿cuántos años tienes?; **old people** los ancianos

old town casco *m* antiguo

on sobre; **on the table** sobre la mesa

once una vez; **once a day/an hour** una vez al día/a la hora

one uno *m*/una *f*

only sólo

open *(adj)* abierto *m*/abierta *f*

open *(v)* abrir

operate operar

operation operación *f*; **to have an operation** ser operado

opinion opinión *f*; **in my opinion** en mi opinión

opportunity oportunidad *f*

opposite *(n)* contrario *m*/contraria

opposite *(prep)* en frente de

optician's óptica *f*

or o

orange naranja *f*

orchestra orquesta *f*

order *(n)* orden; **out of order** averiado

order *(v)* pedir **45**

organic orgánico *m*/orgánica *f*

organize organizar

other otro *m*/otra *f*; **others** otros *mpl*/otras *fpl*

otherwise *(if not)* si no; *(differently)* de otra manera

our nuestro *m*/nuestra *f*, nuestros *mpl*/nuestras *fpl* *(see grammar)*

ours nuestro *m*/nuestra *f* *(see grammar)*

outside fuera

outward journey viaje *m* de ida

oven horno m

over *(prep)* encima; **over there** allí

overdone *(food)* demasiado hecho m/hecha f

overweight demasiado pesado m/pesada f; **my luggage is overweight** tengo exceso de peso

owe deber **79, 104**

own *(adj)* propio m/propia f; **my own car** mi propio coche

own *(v)* ser propietario de

owner propietario m/propietaria f

---

pack empaquetar; **I packed my suitcase** me hice la maleta

package holiday vacaciones fpl organizadas

packed *(place)* lleno m/llena f

packet paquete m

painting cuadro m

pair par m; **a pair of pyjamas** un pijama; **a pair of shorts** un pantalón corto

palace palacio m

pants *(ladies')* bragas fpl; *(men's)* calzoncillos mpl

paper papel m; **paper napkin** servilleta f de papel

parcel paquete m

pardon? ¿cómo?

parents padres mpl

park *(n)* parque m

park *(v)* aparcar

parking space aparcamiento m

part parte f; **to be a part of** ser parte de

party fiesta f

pass *(n)* *(permit)* pase m

pass *(v)* pasar

passenger pasajero m/pasajera f

passport pasaporte m

past pasado; **a quarter past ten** las diez y cuarto

path camino m, sendero m

patient *(n)* paciente mf

pay pagar **79**

pedestrian peatón m/peatona f

pedestrianized street calle f peatonal

pee *(v)* hacer pis

peel pelar

pen *(ballpoint)* bolígrafo m; *(fountain)* pluma f; **do you have a pen?** ¿tienes un boli?

pencil lápiz m

people gente f **44**

percent por ciento

perfect perfecto m/perfecta f

perfume perfume m

perhaps quizás

period *(of time)* periodo m; *(menstruation)* regla f

person persona f

personal stereo walkman® m

petrol gasolina f **29**

petrol station gasolinera f

phone *(n)* teléfono m

phone *(v)* llamar por teléfono, telefonear

phone box cabina f (telefónica) **96**

phone call llamada f telefónica; **to make a phone call** hacer una llamada telefónica

phonecard tarjeta f telefónica **96**

phone number número m de teléfono

photo foto f **84**, **85**; **to take a photo (of)** hacer una foto (de) **84**; **to take someone's photo** hacer una foto de alguien

picnic picnic m; **to have a picnic** hacer un picnic

pie pastel m

piece pieza f, trozo m; **a piece of** un trozo de; **a piece of fruit** una pieza de fruta

piles hemorroides fpl

pill píldora f; **to be on the pill** estar tomando la píldora

pillow almohada f

pillowcase funda f de almohada

PIN (number) número m personal

pink rosa

pity pena: **it's a pity** es una pena

place lugar m, sitio m

plan plan m

plane avión m **25**

plant planta f

plaster cast escayola f

plastic plástico m

plastic bag bolsa f de plástico

plate plato m

platform andén m **27**

play (n) (in theatre) obra m

play (v) (game) jugar; (instrument) tocar

please por favor

pleased encantado m/encantada f; **pleased to meet you!** ¡encantado de conocerte!

pleasure placer m

plug (in bath) tapón m; (electrical) enchufe m

plug in enchufar

plumber fontanero m/fontanera f

point punto m

police policía f

policeman policía m

police station comisaría f **108**

policewoman policía f

poor pobre

port puerto m

portrait retrato m

Portugal Portugal m

Portuguese (adj) portugués m/portuguesa f

Portuguese (n) (person) portugués m/portuguesa f; (language) portugués m

possible posible

post (n) correo m

post (v) mandar por correo

postbox buzón m **89**

postcard postal f

postcode código m postal

poster póster m, cartel m

postman cartero m

post office (Oficina f de) Correos m **89**

pot (for cooking) olla f; (for plants) maceta f

pound libra f

powder polvo m

practical práctico m/práctica f

pram cochecito m (de bebé)

prefer preferir

pregnant embarazada **103**

prepare preparar

present (n) regalo m **83**

press (n) prensa f

pressure presión f

previous previo m/previa f

price precio m

private privado m/privada f

prize premio m

probably probablemente

problem problema m

procession procesión f
product producto m
profession profesión f
programme programa m
promise (v) prometer
propose proponer
protect proteger
proud (of) orgulloso m/orgullosa f (de)
public público m/pública f
public holiday fiesta f oficial
pull tirar
purple morado m/morada f
purpose propósito m; **on purpose** a propósito
purse monedero m
push empujar
pushchair sillita f (de ruedas)
put poner
put out (light, fire) apagar
put up (tent) armar
put up with aguantar

Q

quality cualidad f; **of good/poor quality** de buena/mala calidad
quarter cuarto m; **a quarter of an hour** un cuarto de hora; **a quarter to ten** las diez menos cuarto
quay muelle m
question pregunta f
queue (n) cola f
queue (v) hacer cola
quick rápido m/rápida f
quickly rápidamente
quiet (calm) tranquilo m/tranquila f; (silent) silencioso m/silenciosa f
quite bastante; **quite a lot of flights** bastantes vuelos

R

racist (adj) racista
racket raqueta f
radiator radiador m
radio radio f
radio station emisora f (de radio)
rain (n) lluvia f
rain (v) llover; **it's raining** está lloviendo
raincoat impermeable m
random azar m; **at random** al azar
rape (v) violar
rare (unusal) raro m/rara f; (meat) poco hecho m/hecha f
rarely raramente
rather más bien
raw crudo m/cruda f
razor maquinilla f de afeitar
razor blade hoja f de afeitar
reach alcanzar
read leer
ready preparado m/preparada f, listo m/lista f
reasonable razonable
receipt recibo m **79, 104**
receive recibir
reception recepción f; **at reception** en la recepción **38**
receptionist recepcionista mf
recipe receta f
recognize reconocer
recommend recomendar **36, 43**
red rojo m/roja f; **she has red hair** es pelirroja
red light luz f roja; **to drive through a red light** pasarse el semáforo en rojo
red wine vino m tinto
reduce reducir

reduction *(in price)* rebaja f, descuento m

refrigerator frigorífico m

refund *(n)* devolución f de dinero **82**; **I got a refund** me devolvieron el dinero

refund *(v)* devolver el dinero

refuse negarse

registered *(mail)* certificado m/certificada f

registration number (número m de) matrícula f

remember recordar

remind recordar

remove quitar; **remove your car** llévese el coche

rent *(n)* alquiler m

rent *(v)* alquilar **38**

rental alquiler m

reopen reabrir, abrir de nuevo

repair reparar, arreglar **29**

repeat repetir

reserve reservar

reserved reservado m/reservada f

rest *(n)* *(relaxation)* descanso m; *(remains)* resto m

rest *(v)* descansar

restaurant restaurante m **43**

return *(n)* vuelta f

return ticket billete m de ida y vuelta

reverse-charge call llamada f a cobro revertido **96**

reverse gear marcha f atrás

rheumatism reumatismo m

rib costilla f

right *(n)* *(not left)* derecha f; *(entitlement)* derecho m; **to the right (of)** a la derecha (de); **to have the right to …** tener derecho a …

right *(adj)* *(not left)* derecho m/derecha f; *(correct)* correcto m/correcta f; **all right** de acuerdo; **are you all right?** ¿estás bien?

right *(adv)* justo; **right away** enseguida; **right beside** justo al lado

ring *(n)* *(jewellery)* anrillo m

ring *(v)* llamar

ripe maduro m/madura f

rip-off robo m

risk *(v)* arriesgar

river río m

road carretera f

road sign señal f de tráfico

roadworks obras fpl

rock piedra f

rollerblades patines mpl en línea

room cuarto m; *(in hotel)* habitación f **35**, **36**

rosé wine vino m rosado

round *(adj)* redondo m/redonda f

roundabout rotonda f

rubbish basura f; **to take the rubbish out** sacar la basura

rucksack mochila f

rug alfombra f

ruins ruinas fpl; **in ruins** en ruinas

run out *(come to an end)* agotarse

S

sad triste

safe seguro m/segura f

safety seguridad f

safety belt cinturón m de seguridad

sail *(v)* navegar

sailing navegación f; **to go sailing** salir a navegar

sale venta f; *(low prices)* rebajas fpl;

for sale en venta; **in the sale** en las rebajas
sales rebajas *fpl*
salt sal *f*
salted con sal
salty salado *m*/salada *f*
same mismo *m*/misma *f*; **the same** el mismo **46**
sand arena *f*
sandals sandalias *fpl*
sanitary towel compresa *f*
Saturday sábado *m*
saucepan cacerola *f*; *(big)* olla *f*
save *(v) (money)* ahorrar; *(rescue)* salvar
say decir; **how do you say …?** ¿cómo se dice …?
scared asustado *m*/asustada *f*; **to be scared (of)** tener miedo (de)
scenery paisaje *m*
scissors tijeras *fpl*
scoop *(of ice cream)* bola *f*
scooter *(child's)* patinete *m*; *(motorcycle)* Vespa® *f*
scotch *(whisky)* whisky *m* escocés
Scotland Escocia *f*
Scottish escocés *m*/escocesa *f*
scuba diving submarinismo *m*
sea mar *m*
seafood mariscos *mpl*
seasick mareado *m*/mareada *f*
seaside playa *f*; **at the seaside** en la playa
seaside resort centro *m* de veraneo costero
season temporada *f*
seat asiento *m* **24**
sea view vista *f* al mar
seaweed alga *f* marina
second segundo *m*/segunda *f*
second class segunda clase *f*

secondary school instituto *m*
second-hand de segunda mano
secure seguro *m*/segura *f*
security seguridad *f*
see ver; **see you later!** ¡hasta luego!; **see you soon!** ¡hasta pronto!; **see you tomorrow!** ¡hasta mañana!
seem parecer; **it seems that …** parece que …
seldom raramente
sell vender **77**
Sellotape® celo *m*, cinta *f* adhesiva
send enviar
sender remitente *mf*
sense sentido *m*
sensitive sensible
sentence frase *f*
separate separar
separately por separado
September septiembre *m*
serious *(person)* serio *m*/seria *f*; *(accident, illness)* grave
several varios *mpl*/varias *fpl*
sex sexo *m*
shade *(n)* sombra *f*
shame *(pity)* pena *f*
shampoo champú *m*
shape forma *f*
share *(v)* compartir
shave *(v)* afeitarse
shaving cream crema *f* de afeitar
shaving foam espuma *f* de afeitar
she ella
sheet sábana *f*
shellfish mariscos *mpl*
shirt camisa *f*
shock *(n) (jolt)* choque *m*; *(surprise)* shock *m*, impresión *f*
shocking *(very bad)* horroroso *m*/horrorosa *f*; *(surprising)* chocante

shoes zapatos *mpl*
shop tienda *f*
shop assistant dependiente *mf*
shopkeeper tendero *m*/tendera *f*
shopping compras *fpl*; **to do the shopping** hacer la compra
shopping centre centro *m* comercial
short corto; **I'm two … short** me hacen falta dos …
short cut atajo *m*
shorts pantalón *m* corto
short-sleeved de manga corta
shoulder hombro *m*
show *(n)* espectáculo *m* **62**
show *(v)* mostrar
shower ducha *f*; **to have a shower** ducharse
shower gel gel *m* de baño
shut *(adj)* cerrado *m*/cerrada *f*
shut *(v)* cerrar
shuttle *(air route)* puente *m* aéreo; *(bus)* lanzadera
shy tímido *m*/tímida *f*
sick enfermo *m*/enferma *f*; **to feel sick** tener ganas de vomitar
side lado *m*
sign *(n)* señal *f*
sign *(v) (letter, form)* firmar
signal señal *f*
silence silencio *m*
silver plata *f*
silver-plated plateado *m*/plateada *f*
since desde
sing cantar
singer cantante *mf*
single *(not married)* soltero *m*/soltera *f*; *(room)* individual; **single ticket** billete *m* de ida
sister hermana *f*

sit down sentarse
size tamaño *m*; *(of garment)* talla *f*; *(of shoes)* número *m*; *(of person)* estatura *f*
ski esquiar
ski boots botas *fpl* de esquí
skiing esquí *m*; **to go skiing** esquiar
ski lift telesquí *m*
skin piel *f*
ski resort estación *f* de esquí
ski stick bastón *m*
skirt falda *f*
sky cielo *m*
skyscraper rascacielos *m*
sleep *(n)* sueño *m*
sleep *(v)* dormir; **to sleep with** dormir con
sleeping bag saco *m* de dormir
sleeping pill somnífero *m*
sleeve manga *f*
slice *(of bread)* rebanada *f*; *(of ham)* loncha *f*; *(of beef)* tajada *f*; *(of cake)* trozo *m*
sliced cortado *m*/cortada *f* en rebanadas/lonchas
slide *(v)* resbalarse
slow lento *m*/lenta *f*
slowly lentamente, despacio
small pequeño *m*/pequeña *f*
smell *(n)* olor *m*
smell *(v)* oler; **to smell good/bad** oler bien/mal
smile *(n)* sonrisa *f*
smile *(v)* sonreír
smoke *(n)* humo *m*
smoke *(v)* fumar
smoker fumador *m*/fumadora *f*
snack tapa *f*, tentempié *m*
snow *(n)* nieve *f*
snow *(v)* nevar

so así que; **so that** para que
soap jabón m
soccer fútbol m
socks calcetines mpl
some algún m/alguna f; **some tourists** algunos turistas
somebody, someone alguien
something algo; **something else** algo más
sometimes a veces
somewhere en algún sitio; **somewhere else** en otro sitio
son hijo m
song canción f
soon pronto
sore dolorido m/dolorida f; **to have a sore throat** tener dolor de garganta
sorry! ¡lo siento!, ¡perdón!
south sur m; **in the south** en el sur; **(to the) south of** (al) sur de
souvenir recuerdo m
Spain España f
Spanish (adj) español m/española f
Spanish (n) (language) español m
spare part pieza f de repuesto
spare tyre rueda f de repuesto
spare wheel rueda f de repuesto
spark plug bujía f
speak hablar **8**, **10**, **97**, **108**
special (n) especialidad f; **today's special** plato m del día
speciality especialidad f
speed velocidad f; **at full speed** a máxima velocidad
spell (v) deletrear; **how do you spell it?** ¿cómo se escribe?
spend gastar
spice especia f
spicy picante
spider araña f

splinter astilla f
split up separarse
spoil estropear
sponge esponja f
spoon cuchara f
sport deporte m
sports ground campo m de deportes
sporty deportivo m/deportiva f
spot (place) sitio m; (pimple) grano m
sprain torcerse; **to sprain one's ankle** torcerse el tobillo
spring (season) primavera f
square (n) (in town) plaza f; (shape) cuadrado m
stadium estadio m
stain mancha f
stained-glass windows vidrieras fpl
stairs escaleras fpl
stamp (n) sello m **90**
start (v) empezar
state estado m
statement declaración f
station estación f
stay (n) estancia f
stay (v) quedarse; **to stay in touch** seguir en contacto
steal robar **108**
step (n) (movement) paso m; (of stairs) escalón m
sticking plaster tirita f
still (adv) todavía
still water agua f sin gas
sting (n) (by insect) picadura f; (burning) escozor m
sting (v) (insect) picar **102**; (burn) escocer; **I've been stung by a bee** me ha picado una abeja

stock existencias *fpl*; **out of stock** agotado

stomach estómago *m*

stone *(rock)* piedra *f*; *(in fruit)* hueso *m*

stop *(n)* parada *f* **27**

stop *(v)* parar

storey piso *m*

storm tormenta *f*

straight ahead, straight on todo recto

strange extraño *m*/extraña *f*

street calle *f*

strong fuerte

stuck atascado *m*/atascada *f*

student estudiante *mf*

studies estudios *mpl* **15**

study *(v)* estudiar

style estilo *m*

subtitled subtitulado *m*/subtitulada *f*

suburb barrio *m* periférico

suffer sufrir

suggest sugerir

suit *(n)* traje *m*

suit *(v)* convenir; **does that suit you?** ¿te conviene bien?

suitcase maleta *f*

summer verano *m*

summit cima *f*

sun sol *m*; **in the sun** al sol

sunbathe tomar el sol

sunburnt quemadura *f* (de sol); **to get sunburnt** quemarse

sun cream crema *f* solar

Sunday domingo *m*

sunglasses gafas *fpl*

sunhat sombrero *m*

sunrise amanecer *m*

sunset anochecer *m*

sunstroke insolación *f*; **to get sunstroke** tener una insolación

supermarket supermercado *m* **39**, **77**

supplement suplemento *m*

sure seguro *m*/segura *f*

surf *(v)* *(sport)* surfear, hacer surf

surfboard tabla *f* de surf

surfing surfing *m*; **to go surfing** surfear, hacer surf

surgical spirit alcohol *m*

surname apellido *m*

surprise *(n)* sorpresa *f*

surprise *(v)* sorprender

sweat *(v)* sudar

sweater jersey *m*

sweet *(adj)* dulce

sweet *(n)* caramelo *m*; *(chocolate)* bombón *m*; *(dessert)* postre *m*

swim *(n)* baño *m*; **to go for a swim** darse un baño, nadar

swim *(v)* nadar

swimming natación *m*

swimming pool piscina *f*

swimming trunks bañador *m*

swimsuit traje *m* de baño

switch off apagar

switch on encender

switchboard operator telefonista *mf*

swollen hinchado *m*/hinchada *f*

synagogue sinagoga *f*

syrup jarabe *m*

T

table mesa *f* **44**

tablespoon cuchara *f* de servir

tablet pastilla *f*

take tomar; **it takes 2 hours** se tarda 2 horas

take off *(plane)* despegar

takeaway *(food)* para llevar

talk hablar

tall alto *m*/alta *f*

tampon tampón *m*

tan *(n)* bronceado *m*

tanned bronceado *m*/bronceada *f*, moreno *m*/morena *f*

tap grifo *m*

taste *(n)* sabor *m*

taste *(v)* saber; **to taste good** saber bien

tax impuesto *m*

tax-free libre de impuestos

taxi taxi *m* **30**

taxi driver taxista *mf*

team equipo *m*

teaspoon cucharilla *f*

teenager adolescente *mf*

telephone *(n)* teléfono *m*

telephone *(v)* llamar por teléfono, telefonear

television televisión *f*

tell decir

temperature temperatura *f*; **to have a temperature** tener fiebre **103**; **to take one's temperature** tomarse la temperatura

temple templo *m*

temporary temporal

tennis tenis *m*

tennis court pista *f* de tenis

tennis shoe zapatilla *f* de tenis

tent tienda *f*

tent peg estaca *f*

terminal *(in airport)* terminal *f*

terrace terraza *f*

terrible terrible

thank dar las gracias; **thank you** gracias; **thank you very much** muchas gracias

thanks gracias *fpl*; **thanks to** gracias a

that aquel *m*/aquella *f*; **that one** aquél *m*/aquélla *f*

the el *m*/la *f* *(see grammar)*

theatre teatro *m*

theft robo *m*

their su, sus; **their room** su cuarto; **their passports** sus pasaportes *(see grammar)*

theirs suyo *m*/suya *f* *(see grammar)*

them los, las, les *(see grammar)*

theme park parque *m* temático

then entonces

there allí; **there is** hay **8**; **there are** hay

therefore por tanto

thermometer termómetro *m*

Thermos® flask termo *m*

these estos *mpl*/estas *fpl*; **these ones** éstos *mpl*/éstas *fpl*

they ellos *mpl*/ellas *fpl*; **they say that …** dicen que … *(see grammar)*

thief ladrón *m*/ladrona *f*

thigh muslo *m*

thin delgado *m*/delgada *f*

thing cosa *f*

think pensar; **to think about …** pensar en …

thirsty con sed; **to be thirsty** tener sed

this este *m*/esta *f*; **this one** éste *m*/ésta *f*; **this evening** esta tarde; **this is my husband** éste es mi marido

those aquellos *mpl*/aquellas *fpl*; **those ones** aquéllos *mpl*/aquéllas *fpl*

throat garganta *f*

throw tirar

throw out *(rubbish)* tirar, arrojar; *(person)* echar

Thursday jueves *m*

ticket billete *m* **23**, **62**

ticket office taquilla *f*

tidy ordenado *m*/ordenada *f*

tie *(n)* corbata *f*

tie *(v)* atar

tight apretado *m*/apretada *f*

tights medias *fpl*

time tiempo *m*, hora *f*; **what time is it?** ¿qué hora es?; **from time to time** de vez en cuando; **on time** puntual; **three/four times** tres/cuatro veces

time difference diferencia *f* horaria

timetable horario *m* **23**

tinfoil papel *m* de aluminio

tip propina *f*

tired cansado *m*/cansada *f*

tissue pañuelo *m* de papel

tobacco tabaco *m*

tobacconist's estanco *m*

today hoy

together juntos *m*/juntas *f*

toilet servicio *m*, lavabo *m* **8**, **43**

toilet bag bolsa *f* de aseo, neceser *m*

toilet paper papel *m* higiénico

toiletries artículos *mpl* de aseo

toll peaje *m*

tomorrow mañana; **tomorrow evening** mañana por la tarde; **tomorrow morning** mañana por la mañana

tongue lengua *f*

tonight esta noche

too *(also)* también; *(excessively)* demasiado; **too many** demasiados; **too much** demasiado

tooth diente *m*

toothbrush cepillo *m* de dientes

toothpaste pasta *f* de dientes

top *(upper part)* parte *f* superior; **at the top** en la parte superior

torch linterna *f*

touch tocar

tourist turista *mf*

tourist office oficina *f* de turismo

tourist trap atracción *f* turística

towards hacia

towel toalla *f*

town ciudad *f*

town centre centro *m* (de la ciudad)

town hall ayuntamiento *m*

toy juguete *m*

traditional tradicional

traffic tráfico *m*

traffic jam atasco *m* **29**

train tren *m* **27**; **the train to Seville** el tren de Sevilla

train station estación *f* de tren

tram tranvía *m*

transfer *(n) (of money)* transferencia *f*

translate traducir

travel *(v)* viajar

travel agency agencia *f* de viajes

traveller's cheque cheque *m* de viaje

trip viaje *m*; **have a good trip!** ¡buen viaje!

trolley carrito *m*

trouble problema *m*; **to have trouble doing something** tener problemas para hacer algo

trousers pantalón *m*

true verdadero *m*/verdadera *f*; **it's true** es verdad

try intentar; **to try to do**

something intentar hacer algo
try on probarse **81**
Tuesday martes *m*
tube *(train)* metro *m*
tube station estación *f* de metro
turn *(n)* turno *m*; **it's your turn** te toca
turn *(v)* girar
twice dos veces
type *(n)* tipo *m*
type *(v)* escribir a máquina
typical típico *m*/típica *f*
tyre neumático *m*

U

umbrella paraguas *m*
uncle tío *m*
uncomfortable incómodo *m*/incómoda *f*
under debajo de
underground *(n)* *(tube)* metro *m*
underground line línea *f* de metro
underground station estación *f* de metro
underneath *(prep)* debajo de
understand entender, comprender **10**
underwear ropa *f* interior
United Kingdom Reino Unido *m*
United States Estados Unidos *mpl*
until hasta
upset *(adj)* *(displeased)* disgustado *m*/disgustada *f*; **to have an upset stomach** estar mal del estómago
upstairs arriba
urgent urgente
us nos, a nosotros *(see grammar)*
use usar; **to be used for** usarse

para; **I'm used to it** estoy acostumbrado
useful útil
useless inútil
usually normalmente
U-turn *(on road)* cambio *m* de sentido

V

vaccinated (against) vacunado *m*/vacunada *f* (contra)
valid (for) válido*m*/válida *f* (para)
valley valle *m*
VAT IVA *m*
vegetarian *(adj)* vegetariano *m*/vegetariana *f*
very muy
view vista *f*
villa *(in country)* casa *f* de campo; *(chalet)* chalet *m*
village pueblo *m*
visa *(permit)* visado *m*
visit *(n)* visita *f*
visit *(v)* visitar
volleyball voleibol *m*
vomit vomitar

WXYZ

waist cintura *f*
wait *(v)* esperar; **to wait for something/someone** esperar algo/a alguien
waiter camarero *m*
waitress camarera *f*
wake up despertar(se)
Wales (País *m* de) Gales *m*
walk *(n)* paseo *m* **72**; **to go for a walk** dar un paseo
walk *(v)* andar

walking *(hobby)* senderismo *m*; **to go walking** hacer senderismo

walking boots botas *fpl* de andar

Walkman® walkman®

wallet monedero *m*, cartera *f*

want querer; **to want to do something** querer hacer algo

warm caliente; **it's very warm** *(weather)* hace mucho calor

warn advertir

wash *(n)* lavado *m*; **to have a wash** lavarse

wash *(v)* lavar; **to wash one's hair** lavarse el pelo

washbasin lavabo *m*

washing *(laundry)* colada *f*; **to do the washing** hacer la colada, lavar la ropa

washing machine lavadora *f*

washing powder detergente *m*

washing-up liquid *(detergente m)* lavavajillas *m*

wasp avispa *f*

waste *(v)* malgastar

watch *(n)* reloj *m*

watch *(v)* mirar, observar; **watch out!** ¡cuidado!

water agua *f* **38**, **45**

water heater calentador *m* (de agua)

waterproof impermeable

waterskiing esquí *m* acuático

wave *(in sea)* ola *f*

way *(method)* manera *f*; *(to get somewhere)* camino *m*

way in entrada *f*

way out salida *f*

we nosotros *mpl*/nosotras *fpl* *(see grammar)*

weak débil

wear *(clothes)* llevar

weather tiempo *m* **21**; **the weather's bad** hace mal tiempo

weather forecast pronóstico *m* del tiempo

website sitio *m* web, website *f*

Wednesday miércoles *m*

week semana *f*

weekend fin *m* de semana

welcome bienvenido *m*/bienvenida *f*; **you're welcome** de nada

well bien; **I'm very well** estoy muy bien; **well done** *(meat)* bien hecho *m*/hecha *f*

well-known muy conocido *m*/conocida *f*

Welsh galés *m*/galesa *f*

west oeste *m*; **in the west** en el oeste; **(to the) west of** (al) oeste de

wet mojado *m*/mojada *f*; *(slightly)* húmedo *m*/húmeda *f*; **wet paint** *(sign)* recién pintado

wetsuit traje *m* isotérmico

what qué; **what do you want?** ¿qué quiere?

wheel rueda *f*

wheelchair silla *f* de ruedas

when cuándo

where dónde; **where is/are …?** ¿dónde está/están …?; **where are you from?** ¿de dónde eres?; **where are you going?** ¿dónde vas?

which cuál

while mientras

white blanco *m*/blanca *f*; **white wine** vino blanco

who quién; **who's calling?** ¿de parte de quién?

whole entero m/entera f; **the whole cake** todo el pastel
whose cuyo m/cuya f
why por qué
wide ancho
wife mujer f, esposa f
wild (animal) salvaje; (plant) silvestre
wind viento m
window ventana f; (of shop) escaparate m
windscreen parabrisas m
windsurfing windsurf(ing) m
wine vino m **45, 46**
winter invierno m
with con
withdraw retirar
withdrawal reintegro m
without sin
woman mujer f
wonderful maravilloso m/ maravillosa f
wood (material) madera f; (forest) bosque m
wool lana f
work (n) trabajo m; **work of art** obra f de arte
work (v) trabajar **15**
world mundo m
worse peor; **to get worse** empeorar; **it's worse (than)** es peor (que)

worth: to be worth three euros valer tres euros; **it's worth it** merece la pena
wound (n) herida f
wrist muñeca f
write escribir **10**
wrong equivocado m/equivocada f; **you're wrong** estás equivocado

X-ray (picture) radiografía f

year año m
yellow amarillo m/amarilla f
yes sí
yesterday ayer; **yesterday evening** ayer por la tarde
you tú (see grammar)
young joven
your tu (see grammar)
yours tuyo m/tuya f/tuyos mpl/ tuyas fpl (see grammar)
youth hostel albergue m juvenil

zero cero m
zip cremallera f
zoo zoo m, zoológico m
zoom (lens) zoom m, teleobjetivo m

DICTIONARY

SPANISH-ENGLISH

A

a to
abadía f abbey
abajo downstairs
abanico m fan
abeja f bee
abierto open
abogado m, **abogada** f lawyer
abolladura f bump
abrebotellas m bottle opener
abrelatas m can opener
abrigo m coat
abril m April
abrir to open
acabar to finish, to end; **acabar de ...** to have just ...
acantilado m cliff
acaso: por si acaso just in case
acceso m access
accidente m accident
aceite m oil
aceptar to accept
aconsejar to advise
acostumbrado accustomed, used
acuerdo: de acuerdo in agreement; all right
adaptador m adaptor
adelantado: por adelantado in advance
¡adiós! bye!
admisión f admission
adolescente mf teenager

aduana f customs
advertir to warn
aeropuerto m airport
afección f **gastrointestinal vírica** gastric flu
afeitarse to shave, to have a shave
afortunado lucky
after-sun m after-sun (cream)
agencia f **de viajes** travel agency
agosto m August
agotado exhausted; out of stock
agotarse to run out
agredir to attack
agua f water; **agua con gas** sparkling water; **agua mineral** mineral water; **agua no potable** non-drinking water; **agua potable** drinking water; **agua sin gas** still water
aguantar to put up with, to stand
agujero m hole; leak
ahogarse to drown
ahora now
ahorrar to save (money)
aire m air; **aire acondicionado** air conditioning
al to the; **al cine** to the cinema
albergue m **juvenil** youth hostel
alcanzar to reach
alcohol m alcohol; surgical spirit
alemán German
alemán m, **alemana** f German
Alemania f Germany

alergia *f* **al polen** hay fever
alérgico allergic
alfombra *f* rug, mat
alga *f* **marina** seaweed
algo something; **algo más**
   something else
algodón *m* cotton; **algodón**
   hidrófilo cotton wool
alguien somebody, someone
algún *m*, **alguna** *f* some; **algunos**
   turistas some tourists
aliño *m* salad dressing
allí there
almohada *f* pillow
almorzar to have lunch
almuerzo *m* lunch
alojamiento *m* accommodation
alpinismo *m* climbing
alquilar to let, to rent, to hire
alquiler *m* rent, hire, rental
alrededor de around
alto high, tall; loud
amanecer *m* sunrise, dawn
amarillo yellow
ambos both
ambulancia *f* ambulance
americano American
americano *m*, **americana** *f*
   American
amigo *m*, **amiga** *f* friend
ampolla *f* blister
ancho wide
anciano *m*, **anciana** *f* old man,
   old woman
andar to walk
anestesia *f* anaesthetic
animal *m* animal
aniversario *m* anniversary
anillo *m* ring
anochecer *m* sunset, nightfall
anteayer the day before yesterday

antes before
antibióticos *mpl* antibiotics
anticonceptivo *m* contraceptive
año *m* year; **Año Nuevo** New
   Year; **¿cuántos años tienes?**
   how old are you?
apagar to turn off, to switch off;
   to put out, to extinguish
apagón *m* power cut, blackout
aparcamiento *m* parking space;
   car park
aparcar to park
apartamento *m* flat, apartment
apellido *m* surname
apendicitis *f* appendicitis
aprender to learn
apretado tight
aprovechar: ¡que aproveche!
   enjoy your meal!
aquel *m*, **aquella** *f* that; that one
aquellos *mpl*, **aquellas** *fpl* those;
   those ones
aquí here; **aquí está/están** here
   is/are
araña *f* spider
arena *f* sand
armar to put up *(tent)*
arreglar to arrange; to repair
arriba up; upstairs
arriesgar to risk
arrojar to throw
arte *m* art
artículo *m* item, article; **artículos**
   de aseo toiletries
artista *mf* artist
ascensor *m* lift
aseos *mpl* toilets
así like this, like that; **así que** so;
   así como as well as
asiento *m* seat
asma *m* asthma

aspirina *f* aspirin
astilla *f* splinter
asustado scared, frightened
atacar to attack
atajo *m* short cut
ataque *m* **al corazón** heart attack
atar to tie
atascado stuck, jammed; blocked
atasco *m* traffic jam
atropellar to knock down *(by car)*
aún still, yet
aunque although
autobús *m* bus
autocar *m* coach
autoestop *m* hitchhiking; **hacer autoestop** to hitchhike
autopista *f* motorway
avenida *f* avenue
avería *f* breakdown; **tener una avería** to break down
averiado out of order
avión *m* aeroplane, plane
avispa *f* wasp
ayer yesterday; **ayer por la tarde** yesterday evening
ayuda *f* help; **pedir ayuda** to call for help
ayudar to help
ayuntamiento *m* town hall
azar *m* random; **al azar** at random
azul blue

B

bache *m* hole in the road
bailar to dance
baile *m* dance
bajarse de to get off, to get out of

bajo under; low; **bajo en grasa** low-fat
balcón *m* balcony
banco *m* bank
bañador *m* swimming costume; swimming trunks
baño *m* swim; bath; **darse un baño** to go for a swim; **tomar un baño** to have a bath
bar *m* bar
barato cheap
barba *f* beard
barbacoa *f* barbecue
barbilla *f* chin
barco *m* boat
barrio *m* **periférico** suburb
bastante enough; quite; **¿tienes bastante?** have you got enough?; **bastantes vuelos** quite a lot of flights
bastón *m* stick, ski stick
bastoncillo *m* **(de algodón)** cotton bud
basura *f* rubbish; **sacar la basura** to take the rubbish out
batería *f* battery
bebé *m* baby
beber to drink
bebida *f* drink
biberón *m* baby's bottle
biblioteca *f* library
bici *f* bike
bicicleta *f* bicycle; **bicicleta de montaña** mountain bike
bien well, all right, fine; **¿estás bien?** are you all right?; **estoy bien** I'm fine; **estoy muy bien** I'm very well; **bien hecho** well done *(meat)*
bienvenido welcome

billete m ticket; banknote; **billete de ida** single ticket; **billete de ida y vuelta** return ticket

blanco white

boca f mouth

bol m bowl

bola f ball; scoop (of ice cream)

bolígrafo m ballpoint pen

bolsa f bag; **bolsa de aseo** toilet bag; **bolsa de plástico** plastic bag

bolso m bag, handbag

bomba f **de bicicleta** bicycle pump

bomberos mpl fire brigade

bombilla f light bulb

bombón m chocolate

bombona f **de butano** gas cylinder

bonito beautiful, lovely

borracho drunk

bosque m wood, forest

bota f boot; **botas de andar** walking boots; **botas de esquí** ski boots

botella f bottle

boya f buoy

bragas fpl pants (ladies')

brazo m arm

bronceado tanned, suntanned, brown

bronceado m tan, suntan

bronquitis f bronchitis

bucear to dive, to go diving

buceo m diving

bueno good; **buenos días** good morning; **buenas noches** good evening, good night; **buenas tardes** good afternoon

bujía f spark plug

buscar to look for, to search for

buzón m letterbox, postbox

caballo m horse

cabeza f head

cabina f **(telefónica)** phone box

cacerola f saucepan

cada each, every; **cada uno** each one

cadera f hip

caducado out of date, past its sell-by date

caer(se) to fall

café m café; coffee; **café con leche** latte; **café instantáneo** instant coffee; **café solo** espresso

cafetería f café, cafeteria

caja f checkout, pay desk; box; **caja de ahorros** savings bank; **caja de cambios** gearbox

cajero m **automático** cashpoint

calcetines mpl socks

calefacción f heating

calentador m **(de agua)** water heater

caliente hot; warm

calle f street; **calle peatonal** pedestrianized street

calor m heat; **hace calor** it's hot

calzoncillos mpl underpants

cama f bed

cámara f camera; **cámara digital** digital camera

camarera f waitress

camarero m waiter

cambiar to change; to exchange

cambio m change; exchange; **cambio de sentido** U-turn; **en cambio** on the other hand

camino m path; way

camión m lorry

camisa f shirt
camisón m nightdress
campamento m camp
cámping m campsite; **ir de cámping** to go camping
campismo m camping
campista mf camper
campo m country, countryside; field, pitch; **campo de deportes** sports ground; **campo de golf** golf course
canal m channel; canal
cancelar to cancel
canción f song
cansado tired
cantante mf singer
cantar to sing
capilla f chapel
cara f face
caramelo m sweet
caravana f caravan, camper (vehicle); tailback, hold-up
carné m **de conducir** driving licence
carné m **de identidad** identity card
carnicería f butcher's
caro expensive, dear
carrete m film (for camera)
carretera f road
carril-bici m cycle path
carrito m trolley
carta f letter
cartel m poster
cartera f wallet; briefcase
cartero m postman
casa f house, home; **en casa** at home; **irse a casa** to go home; **casa de campo** villa, cottage
casado married
casco m helmet; **casco antiguo** old town

casi almost, nearly
caso m case; **en caso de duda** in case of doubt
castaño brown
castillo m castle
catedral f cathedral
causa: a causa de because of
CD m CD
celo m Sellotape®
cementerio m cemetery
cena f dinner, supper, evening meal
cenar to have dinner, to have supper
cenicero m ashtray
centímetro m centimetre
centro m centre; **centro comercial** shopping centre; **centro de la ciudad** town centre
cepillo m brush; **cepillo de dientes** toothbrush
cerca near, close; **cerca de ...** near ..., close to ...
cercano near, nearby
cerilla f match
cero m zero
cerrado closed, shut
cerrar to close, to shut; **cerrar con llave** to lock
certificado registered
cerveza f beer
césped m grass, lawn
chalet m chalet, detached house, villa
champú m shampoo
chanclas fpl flip-flops
chaqueta f jacket
cheque m cheque; **cheque de viaje** traveller's cheque
chica f girl
chichón m lump, swelling

hico *m* boy
himenea *f* chimney
hocante shocking, amazing
hocolate *m* chocolate
hoque *m* shock
ibercafé *m* Internet café
iclomotor *m* moped
iego blind
ielo *m* sky; heaven
igarrillo *m* cigarette
ima *f* summit
ine *m* cinema
inta *f* **adhesiva** Sellotape®
intura *f* waist
inturón *m* belt; **cinturón de seguridad** safety belt
irco *m* circus
ita *f* appointment; **pedir una cita** to make an appointment
iudad *f* city, town
laro light; **azul claro** light blue; **¡claro!** of course
lase *f* class; **clase turista** economy class
lave *f* **de entrada** door code
lavo *m* nail *(metal)*
lima *m* climate
obrar to charge
Coca-cola® Coke®
oche *m* car
ochecito *m* **(de bebé)** pram
ocina *f* kitchen; cooking; **cocina de cámping** camping stove
ocinar to cook
ódigo *m* **postal** postcode
oger to catch, to take, to get
ola *f* queue; **hacer cola** to queue
olada *f* washing; **hacer la colada** to do the washing
olchón *m* mattress

colección *f* collection
colina *f* hill
color *m* colour
comer to eat; to have lunch
comida *f* food; meal; lunch; **comida para llevar** takeaway; **cómida rápida** fast food; **hacer la comida** to do the cooking
comisaría *f* police station
comisión *f* commission
como like
cómo how; **¿cómo?** pardon?; **¿cómo estás?** how are you?
cómodo comfortable
compañía *f* company; **compañía aérea** airline
compartimento *m* compartment
compartir to share
compra *f* shopping; **hacer la compra** to do the shopping
comprar to buy
comprender to understand
compresa *f* sanitary towel
comprobar to check
con with; **con gas** fizzy; **con sal** salted
concierto *m* concert
condón *m* condom
conducir to drive
conexión *f* connection
confianza *f* **en si mismo** self-confidence
confirmar to confirm
congelador *m* freezer
conocer to know; to meet; **la conocí ayer** I met her yesterday
conseguir to achieve, to manage to; to get
consejo *m* piece of advice; **pedir consejo a alguien** to ask someone's advice

consigna f left-luggage (office)
construir to build
consulado m consulate
contactar to contact
contacto m contact
contador m meter; **contador de la luz** electricity meter
contagioso contagious
contar to count
contestador m **automático** answering machine
contra against
convenir to suit; **¿te conviene bien?** does that suit you?
copa f cup (trophy); glass; drink; **tomar una copa** to have a drink; **ir a tomar una copa** to go for a drink
corazón m heart
corbata f tie
correcto right, correct
correo m post, mail; **correo aéreo** airmail; **correo electrónico** e-mail
correos m post office
cortar to cut; **cortar en rebanadas/lonchas** to slice; **cortarse** to cut oneself
corto short
cosa f thing
costa f coast
costar to cost; **¿cuánto cuesta?** how much does it cost?
costilla f rib
crecer to grow
creer to believe; to think
crema f cream; **crema de afeitar** shaving cream; **crema hidratante** moisturizer; **crema solar** sun cream
cremallera f zip

cristal m glass; crystal; lens (of glasses)
crucero m cruise
crudo raw
cruz f cross
cruzar to cross, to go across
cuaderno m notebook
cuadrado m square (shape)
cuadro m painting
¿cuál? which?
cualidad f quality; **de buena/mala calidad** of good/poor quality
cualquier any; **cualquier cosa** anything
cualquiera anybody, anyone
cuándo when
¿cuánto? how much?
¿cuántos? how many
cuarto m quarter; **un cuarto de hora** a quarter of an hour; **las diez menos cuarto** a quarter to ten
cuarto m room; **cuarto de baño** bathroom
cubito m **de hielo** ice cube
cubo m bin; **cubo de la basura** dustbin
cubrir to cover
cucaracha f cockroach
cuchara f spoon; **cuchara de servir** tablespoon
cucharilla f teaspoon
cuchillo m knife
cuello m neck
cuenco m bowl
cuenta f bill
cuerpo m body
¡cuidado! watch out!, careful!
cuidar to look after
cumpleaños m birthday

cuyo m, **cuya** f whose

---

dañado damaged
dar to give
de of; from; **de ... a ...** from ... to ...
debajo de below, under, underneath
deber to owe; must; **¿qué le debo?** how much do I owe you?; **deben de ser las cinco** it must be 5 o'clock; **debo irme** I have to go
débil weak
decir to say, to tell; **¿cómo se dice ...?** how do you say ...?
declaración f statement
declarar to declare
dedo m finger
defecto m flaw
dejar to let, to allow, to permit; to leave, to quit
delante de in front of
deletrear to spell
delgado thin
delicatessen m delicatessen, deli
demasiado too; too much; **demasiado hecho** overdone
demasiados too many
dentista mf dentist
dentro in, inside, within
departamento m department
depender to depend; **depende (de)** that depends (on)
dependiente mf shop assistant
deporte m sport
deportivo sporty
derecha f right; **a la derecha (de)** to the right (of)

derecho m right; **tener derecho a ...** to have the right to ...
desastre m disaster
desayunar to have breakfast
desayuno m breakfast
descansar to rest
descanso m rest
descuento m discount, concession; **hacerle a alguien un descuento** to give someone a discount
desde from, since
desechable disposable
desinfectar to disinfect
desmayarse to faint
desmayo m blackout; **sufrir un desmayo** to faint
desnudo naked, nude
desodorante m deodorant
despacio slowly
despegar to take off
despertador m alarm clock
despertar(se) to wake up
después later; **después de** after
detrás: detrás de at the back of, behind
devolución f **de dinero** refund
devolver to return, to give back; **devolver el dinero** to refund one's money; **devolver la llamada** to call back
día m day
diabetes f diabetes
diabético diabetic
diarrea f diarrhoea
diciembre m December
diente m tooth
diesel m diesel

dieta *f* diet; **estar a dieta** to be on a diet

diferencia *f* **horaria** time difference

diferente (de) different (from)

difícil difficult

dinero *m* money; **dinero en efectivo** cash

dirección *f* address; direction

directo direct

dirigir to direct; to manage

discoteca *f* disco, nightclub

disculpa *f* excuse *(n)*

disfrutar to enjoy

disgustado upset

disponible available

divertirse to have fun, to enjoy oneself

documentos *mpl* **de identidad** identity papers

doler to hurt; **me duele** it hurts; **me duele la cabeza** I've got a headache

dolor *m* pain, ache; **dolor de cabeza** headache; **tener dolor de garganta** to have a sore throat

dolorido painful, sore

domingo *m* Sunday

¿dónde? where?; **¿dónde está/están …?** where is/are …?

dormir to sleep

droga *f* drug

ducha *f* shower

ducharse to have a shower

dulce sweet

durante during

durar to last

duro hard

SPAN-ENG DICTIONARY

E

echar to throw out

edad *f* age

edificio *m* building

él he; **él mismo** himself *(see grammar)*

el *m* the *(see grammar)*

electricidad *f* electricity

eléctrico electric

ella she *(see grammar)*

ello it *(see grammar)*

ellos *mpl*, **ellas** *fpl* they *(see grammar)*

email *m* e-mail, e-mail address; **mandar un email a alguien** to e-mail someone

embajada *f* embassy

embarazada pregnant

embarque *m* boarding

embrague *m* clutch

emergencia *f* emergency

emisora *f* **(de radio)** radio statio...

empaste *m* filling

empeorar to get worse

empezar to begin, to start

empujar to push

en in; on; **en Inglaterra/2007/ español** in England/2007/Spanish; **en la mesa** on the table

encantado pleased; **¡encantado de conocerte!** pleased to meet you!

encender to light; to turn on, to switch on

enchufar to plug in

enchufe *m* electrical socket

encima de over, above; on

encontrar to find; to meet, to bump into

enero *m* January

nfermedad f illness

nfermero m, **enfermera** f nurse

nfermo ill

nseguida right away

ntender to understand

ntero whole, complete

ntonces then

ntrada f entrance, way in

ntrar to come in; to go in

ntre among, between

nviar to send

piléptico epileptic

quipaje m baggage, luggage; **equipaje de mano** hand luggage

quipo m equipment, team

quivocado wrong; mistaken; **estás equivocado** you're wrong

rror m mistake; **cometer un error** to make a mistake

scaleras fpl stairs

scalón m step (of stairs)

scaparate m shop window

scape m leak

scayola f plaster cast

scocer to sting, to burn

scocés Scottish

scocés m, **escocesa** f Scot; Scotsman, Scotswoman

scocia f Scotland

scozor m sting, burning sensation

scribir to write; **escribir a máquina** to type; **¿cómo se escribe?** how do you spell it?

scuchar to listen

spalda f back

spaña f Spain

spañol Spanish

spañol m, **española** f Spaniard

specia f spice

especialidad f speciality

espectáculo m show

espejo m mirror

esperar to wait; to hope; to expect; **¡espere!** hold on!

espiral f coil (contraceptive)

esponja f sponge

esposa f wife

esposo m husband

espuma f **de afeitar** shaving foam

esquí m skiing; ski; **esquí acuá-tico** waterskiing

esquiar to ski

esquina f corner

estaca f tent peg

estación f station; **estación de autobuses** bus station; **estación de esquí** ski resort; **estación de metro** tube station, underground station; **estación de tren** train station

estadio m stadium

estado m state; **Estados Unidos** United States

estancia f stay

estanco m tobacconist's

estar to be (see grammar)

estatura f build (of person)

este m east

este m, **esta** f this

éste m, **ésta** f this, this one

estilo m style

estómago m stomach

estos mpl, **estas** fpl these

éstos mpl, **éstas** fpl these, these ones

estreñido constipated

estropeado damaged, ruined

estropear to spoil, to ruin

estudiante mf student

estudiar to study

estudios *mpl* studies
estupendo great
euro *m* euro
eurocheque *m* Eurocheque
Europa *f* Europe
europeo *m*, **europea** *f* European
excepcional exceptional
excepto except
exceso *m* **de equipaje** excess baggage
existencias *fpl* stock
exposición *f* exhibition
expreso *m* express train
extranjero foreign
extranjero *m*, **extranjera** *f* foreigner; **en el extranjero** abroad
extraño strange

F

fácil easy
factura *f* bill
facturación *f* check-in
facturar to check in
falda *f* skirt
faltar to be missing; **faltan dos …** there are two … missing
familia *f* family
fan *m* fan *(of band)*
farmacia *f* chemist's; **farmacia de guardia** duty chemist's
faro *m* headlight; lighthouse
favor *m* favour
favorito favourite
fax *m* fax
febrero *m* February
fecha *f* date; **fecha de caducidad** expiry date; **fecha de nacimiento** date of birth
feliz happy
feria *f* fair *(n)*

ferry *m* ferry
festival *m* festival
fianza *f* deposit
fiebre *f* fever; **tener fiebre** to have a temperature
fiesta *f* party, festival; **fiesta nacional** national holiday; **fiesta oficial** public holiday
fin *m* end; **fin de semana** weekend
final last, final
final *m* end; **al final de** at the end of
finalmente finally
firmar to sign
flash *m* flash
folleto *m* brochure, leaflet
fondo *m* bottom
fontanero *m*, **fontanera** *f* plumber
footing *m* jogging
forma *f* shape; **de todas formas** anyway
foto *f* photo
fractura *f* fracture
frágil fragile
francés French
francés *m*, **francesa** *f* Frenchman, Frenchwoman
Francia *f* France
frasco *m* bottle
frase *f* sentence
freír to fry
frenar to brake
freno *m* brake; **freno de mano** handbrake
frente *f* forehead; **en frente de** opposite
fresco cool
frigorífico *m* fridge, refrigerator
frío chilly, cold; **hace frío** it's cold; **tengo frío** I'm cold

ito fried
uego *m* fire; **fuegos artificiales**
fireworks; **¿tienes fuego?** do you
have a light?
uera outside
uerte strong
umador *m*, **fumadora** *f* smoker
umar to smoke
unda *f* **de almohada** pillowcase
usible *m* fuse
útbol *m* football, soccer

gafas *fpl* glasses; **gafas de sol**
sunglasses
galería *f* gallery
Gales *m* Wales
galés *m*, **galesa** *f* Welsh
garaje *m* garage
garantía *f* guarantee
garganta *f* throat
gas *m* gas
gasa *f* gauze
gasolina *f* petrol; **gasolina súper**
four-star petrol
gasolinera *f* petrol station
gastar to spend
gay *mf* gay
gel *m* **de baño** shower gel
gemelos *mpl* twins; binoculars
general general
gente *f* people
ginecólogo *m*, **ginecóloga** *f*
gynaecologist
girar to turn
giro *m* **postal internacional**
international money order
golf *m* golf
golpe *m* blow, knock, bump; shock
gordo fat
gotas *fpl* drops

gotera *f* leak
gracias *fpl* thanks; **gracias a**
thanks to; **muchas gracias** thank
you very much; **dar las gracias**
to thank
grado *m* degree
gramos *mpl* grams
Gran Bretaña *f* Great Britain
grande big; **grandes almacenes**
department store
grano *m* spot, pimple
gratis free
grave serious
Grecia *f* Greece
griego *m*, **griega** *f* Greek
grifo *m* tap
gripe *f* flu
gris grey
guapo good-looking, beautiful
guardarropía *f* cloakroom
guía *f* guidebook; **guía del ocio**
listings magazine; **guía telefónica**
directory
guía *mf* guide *(person)*
gustar to like; **eso no me gusta**
I don't like that; **me gustaría …**
I'd like …

habitación *f* room
hablar to speak, to talk
hacer to make; to do
hachís *m* hashish
hacia towards; **hacia adelante**
forward
hambre *m* hunger; **tener
hambre** to be hungry
hambriento hungry
harto fed up; **estar harto (de)**
to be fed up (with)

hasta until, till; **¡hasta luego!** see you later!; **¡hasta pronto!** see you soon!; **¡hasta mañana!** see you tomorrow!
hay there is, there are
hecho *m* fact; **de hecho** in fact; **hecho a mano** hand-made
hemorroides *fpl* piles
herida *f* wound, cut
herido injured, wounded
hermana *f* sister
hermano *m* brother
hielo *m* ice
hierba *f* herb; grass
hígado *m* liver
hija *f* daughter
hijo *m* son
hincha *m* fan, supporter
hinchado swollen
hipertensión *f* high blood pressure
hoja *f* leaf; sheet of paper; **hoja de afeitar** razor blade
¡hola! hi!, hello!
Holanda *f* Holland
hombre *m* man
hombro *m* shoulder
homosexual *mf* homosexual
honesto honest
hora *f* hour; time; **una hora y media** an hour and a half; **¿qué hora es?** what time is it?; **hora de cierre** closing time; **hora local** local time
horario *m* timetable
hormiga *f* ant
horno *m* oven
horroroso shocking, awful
hospital *m* hospital
hotel *m* hotel
hoy today; **hoy en día** nowadays
hueso *m* stone *(in fruit)*

huésped *mf* guest
húmedo damp, wet
humo *m* smoke *(n)*
humor *m* mood; **estar de buen/mal humor** to be in a good/bad mood

I

idioma *m* language
iglesia *f* church
igual the same; **me da igual** I don't mind
impermeable waterproof
impermeable *m* raincoat
importante important
importar to matter; to mind; **no importa** it doesn't matter; **no me importa** I don't mind
impresión *f* impression; shock
impuesto *m* tax
incluido included
incómodo uncomfortable
independiente independent
individual single *(room)*
infección *f* infection
información *f* information; **información telefónica** directory enquiries
Inglaterra *f* England
inglés English
inglés *m*, **inglesa** *f* Englishman, Englishwoman
insecticida *m* insecticide
insecto *m* insect
insolación *f* sunstroke; **tener una insolación** to get sunstroke
insomnio *m* insomnia
instituto *m* secondary school
intención *f* intention; **tener la intención de …** to intend to …
intentar to try, to attempt

ntermitente m indicator
nternacional international
nternet f Internet
ntoxicación f **alimentaria** food poisoning
nútil useless
nvierno m winter
nvitar to invite
nyección f injection
r to go; **ir a buscar** to fetch, to go and get
Irlanda f Ireland
rlandés Irish
rlandés m, **irlandesa** f Irishman, Irishwoman
rse to leave, to go away
isla f island
Italia f Italy
italiano Italian
italiano m, **italiana** f Italian
IVA m VAT
izquierda f left

J

jabón m soap
jarabe m syrup
jardín m garden; **jardín botánico** botanical garden
jarra f jug
jersey m jumper, sweater
¡Jesús! bless you!
jetlag m jetlag
joven young
joven mf young person
joyería f jeweller's; jewellery
juego m game
jueves m Thursday
jugar to play
jugo m juice
juguete m toy
julio m July

junio m June
juntos together
justo just; right; fair; **justo en medio** right in the middle; **no es justo** it's not fair

K

kayak m kayak
kilómetro m kilometre

L

la f the (see grammar)
labio m lip
lado m side; **al lado de** at the side of, beside
ladrón m, **ladrona** f thief
lago m lake
lámpara f lamp
lana f wool
lanzadera f shuttle (bus)
lápiz m pencil
largo long
las the; them (see grammar)
lata f can, tin
lavabo m washbasin; toilet
lavado m wash
lavadora f washing machine
lavandería f launderette
lavar to wash; **lavarse** to have a wash; **lavarse el pelo** to wash one's hair
lavavajillas m dishwasher; washing-up liquid
leer to read
lejos far, a long way
lengua f tongue; language
lentamente slowly
lente f lens; **lentes de contacto** contact lenses
lentillas fpl contact lenses

lento slow
levantarse to get up
libra *f* pound
libre free, available; **libre de impuestos** tax-free
librería *f* bookshop; bookshelf
libro *m* book
limpiar to clean
limpieza *f* **en seco** dry cleaner's
limpio clean
línea *f* line; **línea de autobús** bus route; **línea de metro** underground line
linterna *f* torch
lista *f* list
listo ready
litro *m* litre
llamada *f* call; **llamada a cobro revertido** reverse-charge call; **llamada telefónica** phone call
llamar to ring, call, phone; to call; **¿cómo te llamas?** what's your name?; **llamar por teléfono** to telephone
llano flat
llave *f* key
llegada *f* arrival
llegar to arrive
llenar to fill
lleno full, packed
llevar to wear; to carry
llorar to cry
llover to rain
lluvia *f* rain
¡lo siento! sorry!
loncha *f* slice
los the; them *(see grammar)*
lucha *f* fight
lugar *m* place
lujo *m* luxury
lujoso luxury

luna *f* moon; **luna de miel** honeymoon
lunes *m* Monday
Luxemburgo *m* Luxembourg
luz *f* light; **luz roja** red light

M

maceta *f* plantpot
madera *f* wood
madre *f* mother
maduro ripe
magnífico great
mal, malo bad
maleta *f* suitcase, case; **hacer la maleta** to pack
maletero *m* boot *(of car)*
malgastar to waste
manager *mf* manager
mancha *f* stain
manera *f* way, method
manga *f* sleeve; **de manga corta** short-sleeved
mano *f* hand; **de segunda mano** second-hand
manta *f* blanket
mantener to keep, to maintain
mañana *f* morning; tomorrow; **mañana por la tarde** tomorrow evening; **mañana por la mañana** tomorrow morning
mapa *m* map
máquina *f* machine; **máquina de afeitar** electric shaver; **máquina de lavar** washing machine; **máquina de fotos** camera
maquinilla *f* **de afeitar** razor
mar *m* sea
maravilloso wonderful
marcha *f* **atrás** reverse gear
marea *f* tide; **marea alta** high

tide; **marea baja** low tide
mareado seasick; dizzy
marido m husband
mariscos mpl seafood, shellfish
marrón brown
martes m Tuesday
marzo m March
más more, most; **el más barato** the cheapest one; **el más caro** the most expensive one; **más que** more than; **mucho más** much more; **más bien** rather
matar to kill
mayo m May
me me; **me miró** she looked at me
mechero m lighter
mediano medium, medium-sized
medianoche f midnight
medias fpl tights
medicamentos mpl medicine
medicina f medicine
médico m, **médica** f doctor; **médico cabecera** GP
medio half; middle; **en medio (de)** in the middle (of); **medio litro/kilo** half a litre/kilo
mediodía m midday, noon
mejor better, best; **el mejor** the best; **es mejor ...** it's better to ...
mejorar to get better, to improve
menos less; least; the least; **al menos** at least
mensaje m message
menú m menu
menudo: a menudo often
mercado m market
mes m month
mesa f table
metro m metre; **el metro** the tube, the underground
mezquita f mosque

mi my (see grammar)
microondas m microwave
miedo: tener miedo (de) to be scared (of)
miembro m member
mientras while
miércoles m Wednesday
minusválido disabled
minuto m minute
mío m mine, **mía** f (see grammar)
mirar to look at, to watch
misa f mass
mismo same
mochila f backpack, rucksack
moderno modern
mojado wet
molestar to disturb; **no molestar** do not disturb
molino m mill
momento m moment
monasterio m monastery
moneda f coin; currency
monedero m purse, wallet
montaña f mountain
montañismo m climbing
monumento m monument
morado purple
mordedura f bite
morder to bite
moreno dark-skinned; brown, tanned
morir to die
mosca f fly
mosquito m mosquito
mostrar to show
moto f motorbike
motocicleta f motorbike
motor m engine
móvil m mobile (phone)
mucho a lot; **mucha gente** a lot of people

muelle *m* quay
muerto dead
mujer *f* woman; wife
multa *f* fine
mundo *m* world
muñeca *f* wrist
músculo *m* muscle
museo *m* museum
música *f* music
muslo *m* thigh; leg *(of chicken)*
muy very; **muy conocido** well-known

N

nada nothing; **de nada** you're welcome
nadar to swim
nadie nobody
naranja *f* orange
nariz *f* nose
natación *f* swimming
naturaleza *f* nature
navegación *f* sailing
navegar to sail, to go sailing
necesario necessary
neceser *m* toilet bag
necesitar to need
negarse to refuse
negro black
nervioso nervous
neumático *m* tyre
nevar to snow
ni … ni … neither … nor …; **ni idea** no idea
nieve *f* snow
ninguno no; none
niño *m*, **niña** *f* child
no no; not *(see grammar)*; **no lo sé** I don't know

no fumador *m*, **no fumadora** *f* non-smoker
noche *f* night; evening; **esta noche** tonight
nombre *m* name; **nombre de pila** first name; **nombre de soltera** maiden name
normalmente usually
norte *m* north
nos us *(see grammar)*
nosotros *mpl*, **nosotras** *fpl* we, us *(see grammar)*
nota *f* note
noticias *fpl* news
novela *f* novel
novia *f* girlfriend
noviembre *m* November
novio *m* boyfriend
nuestro *m*, **nuestra** *f*, **nuestros** *mpl*, **nuestras** *fpl* our *(see grammar)*
nuestro *m*, **nuestra** *f* ours *(see grammar)*
nuevo new; **de nuevo** again
número *m* number; size *(shoes)*; **número de matrícula** registration number; **número de teléfono** phone number; **número personal** PIN (number)
nunca never

O

o or
obra *f* work; **obra de arte** work of art; **obra de teatro** play; **obras** works, roadworks
observar to watch, to observe
obvio obvious
océano *m* ocean
octubre *m* October
ocupado busy; engaged

ocurrir to happen
odiar to hate
oeste m west
oferta f offer
oficina f office; **oficina de correos** post office; **oficina de turismo** tourist office
ofrecer to offer
oír to hear
ojo m eye
ola f wave (in sea)
oler to smell
olla f cooking pot; pan
olor m smell (n)
operación f operation
operar to operate
opinión f opinion
oportunidad f opportunity
óptica f optician's
orden order
ordenado tidy
ordenador m computer; **ordenador portátil** laptop
oreja f ear
orgánico organic
organizar to organize
orgulloso (de) proud (of)
orquesta f orchestra
oscuro dark; **azul oscuro** dark blue
otoño m autumn
otro another; other

P

paciente mf patient
padre m father
padres mpl parents
pagar to pay
país m country
paisaje m landscape, scenery

País de Gales m Wales
Países Bajos mpl Netherlands
palacio m palace
pan m bread
panadería f baker's
pantalón m trousers; **pantalón corto** shorts
pañal m nappy
paño m **de cocina** dish towel
pañuelo m handkerchief; **pañuelo de papel** tissue
papel m paper; **papel de aluminio** tinfoil; **papel de fumar** cigarette paper; **papel de regalo** gift wrap; **papel higiénico** toilet paper **paquete** m packet, parcel
par m pair
para for; **para que** so that
parabrisas m windscreen
parachoques m bumper
parada f stop; **parada de autobuses** bus stop
paraguas m umbrella
parar to stop
parecer to seem, to appear
parecerse a to look like
parking m car park
parque m park; **parque de atracciones** funfair; **parque temático** theme park
parte f part; **parte delantera** front; **parte superior** top; **en todas partes** everywhere
partido m match; political party
pasado last; past; **el año pasado** last year; **pasado mañana** the day after tomorrow
pasajero m, **pasajera** f passenger
pasaporte m passport
pasar to pass; to happen
Pascua f Easter

pase *m* pass, permit
paseo *m* walk; **dar un paseo** to go for a walk
paso *m* step *(movement)*
pasta *f* **de dientes** toothpaste
pastel *m* cake; pie
pastilla *f* tablet
pastor *m*, **pastora** *f* minister *(of the church)*; shepherd, shepherdess
pata *f* leg
patines *mpl* **en línea** rollerblades
patinete *m* (child's) scooter
pato *m* duck
peaje *m* toll
peatón *m*, **peatona** *f* pedestrian
pecho *m* chest
pedazo *m* bit
pedir to order; to ask for; **pedir prestado** to borrow
peine *m* comb
pelar to peel
película *f* film, movie
peligroso dangerous
pelirrojo red-haired
pelo *m* hair
peluquero *m*, **peluquera** *f* hairdresser
pena *f* shame, pity; **es una pena** it's a pity
pendientes *mpl* earrings
pensar to think
pensión *f* boarding-house, guest house; hostel; **pensión completa** full board; **media pensión** half board
peor worse, worst
pequeño little, small
perchero *m* coathanger
perder to lose; to miss; **he perdido mis llaves** I've lost my

keys; **perdimos el ferry** we missed the ferry
perder to lose
¡perdón! sorry!
perdonar to excuse; **perdona** excuse me
perfecto perfect
perfume *m* perfume
periódico *m* newspaper
periodo *m* period
permitir to allow, to permit, to le
pero but
persona *f* person
pesado heavy; boring
pescadería *f* fishmonger's, fish shop
pescado *m* fish
picadura *f* sting; bite
picante spicy, hot
picar to bite; to sting; to be spicy
picnic *m* picnic
pie *m* foot
piedra *f* rock, stone
piel *f* skin
pierna *f* leg
pieza *f* piece; **pieza de repuesto** spare part
pila *f* battery
píldora *f* pill; **píldora del día después** morning-after pill
pinchazo *m* puncture
pis: hacer pis to (have a) pee
piscina *f* swimming pool
piso *m* flat, apartment; storey
pista *f* **de tenis** tennis court
placa *f* **de cocina** hotplate
placer *m* pleasure
plan *m* plan
plancha *f* iron *(n)*
planchar to iron
planta *f* plant; floor, storey;

planta baja ground floor

plástico m plastic

plata f silver

plataforma f platform

plateado silver-plated

plato m plate; dish; course; **plato del día** today's special; **plato principal** main course; **lavar los platos** to do the dishes

playa f beach; seaside; **en la playa** on the beach, at the seaside

plaza f square (in a town)

pluma f fountain pen

pobre poor

poco little, not much; **poco hecho** rare (meat)

pocos few

poder can, be able to; might; **puede ser que llueva** it might rain

policía f police; policewoman

policía m policeman

polvo m powder

pomada f ointment

poner to put

por for; by; **por ciento** percent; **por favor** please; **¿por qué?** why?; **por separado** separately; **por tanto** so, therefore; **por carretera** by road

Portugal m Portugal

portugués Portuguese

portugués m, **portuguesa** f Portuguese

posible possible

postal f postcard

póster m poster

postre m dessert, sweet

práctico practical

precio m price, fare, charge; **precio completo** full fare, full price

preferir to prefer

prefijo m dialling code

pregunta f question

preguntar to ask

premio m prize

prensa f press

preparado ready

preparar to prepare

prestar to lend

previo previous

primavera f spring

primero first; **primera clase** first class; **primera planta** first floor; **en primer lugar** first of all

principal main

principiante mf beginner

principio m beginning

prisa f hurry; **darse prisa** to hurry; **tener prisa** to be in a hurry

prismáticos mpl binoculars

privado private

probablemente probably

probador m fitting room

probarse to try on

problema m problem; **tener problemas para hacer algo** to have trouble doing something

procesión f procession

producto m product; **productos** goods

profesión f profession

profundo deep

programa m programme

prohibido forbidden

prometer to promise

prometida f fiancée

prometido m fiancé

pronóstico m forecast; **pronóstico del tiempo** weather forecast

pronto soon

propietario m, **propietaria** f owner
propina f tip
propio own; **mi propio coche** my own car
proponer to propose
propósito m purpose
proteger to protect
público public
pueblo m village
puente m bridge; **puente aéreo** shuttle service
puerta f door; gate
puerto m port, harbour; **puerto deportivo** marina
pulmón m lung
punto m point; **en punto** o'clock; **las tres en punto** three o'clock; **en su punto** medium (meat); **estar a punto de hacer algo** to be about to do something
puro m cigar

que that; which
¿qué? what?; **¿qué quiere?** what do you want?
quedar to arrange to meet; to be left, to remain; **quedarse** to stay
queja f complaint
quejarse to complain
quemadura f burn
quemar to burn; **quemarse** to get burnt, to burn oneself
querer to want; to love; **querer decir** to mean; **¿qué quiere decir ...?** what does ... mean?
querido dear
¿quién? who?; **¿de parte de quién?** who's calling?

quiosco m **de prensa** newsstand
quitar to remove
quizás maybe, perhaps

racista racist
radiador m radiator
radio f radio
radiografía f X-ray
rápidamente quickly
rápido fast, quick
raqueta f racket
raramente seldom, rarely
raro rare, uncommon; unusual, strange; **raras veces** seldom, rarely
rascacielos m skyscraper
ratón m mouse
razonable reasonable
reabrir to reopen
realidad: en realidad in fact
rebaja f reduction; **rebajas** sales
rebanada f slice
recepción f reception
recepcionista mf receptionist
receta f recipe
recibir to receive
recibo m receipt
recién pintado wet paint
recogida f collection
recomendar to recommend
reconocer to recognize
recordar to remember; to remind
recuerdo m souvenir
redondo round
reducido reduced
reducir to reduce
refugio m **de montaña** mountain hut
regalo m present, gift

172

egla f period *(menstruation)*
Reino Unido m United Kingdom
eintegro m withdrawal
eírse to laugh
ellenar to fill in, to fill out *(form)*;
to fill up
eloj m watch
emitente mf sender
emontarse a to date from
eparar to repair
epetir to repeat
epostar to fill up with petrol
esaca f hangover
esbalarse to slide, to slip
eservado reserved
eservar to book, to reserve
esfriado m cold; **estar**
resfriado to have a cold
esponder to answer
espuesta f answer
estaurante m restaurant
esto m rest
etirar to withdraw
etrasado delayed
etraso m delay
etrato m portrait
eumatismo m rheumatism
eunión f meeting
evelar to develop *(film)*
eventar to burst
evista f magazine
iñón m kidney
ío m river
obar to steal
obo m rip-off; theft
odilla f knee
ojo red
omper to break
opa f clothes; **ropa interior**
underwear
osa pink

rosa f rose
roto broken
rotonda f roundabout
rueda f wheel; **rueda de**
repuesto spare wheel
ruido m noise
ruidoso noisy
ruinas fpl ruins

S

sábado m Saturday
sábana f sheet
saber to know, to know how; to
taste; **no sé** I don't know; **saber**
bien to taste good
sabor m flavour, taste
sacacorchos m corkscrew
saco m **de dormir** sleeping bag
sal f salt
sala f hall; room; **sala de**
conciertos concert hall; **sala de**
estar living room
salado salted, salty
salida f departure, exit, way
out; **salida de emergencia**
emergency exit
salir to leave, to come out, to
go out
salud f health; **¡salud!** cheers!
salvaje wild
salvar to save, to rescue
sandalias fpl sandals
sangrar to bleed
sangre f blood
sartén f frying pan
secador m **de pelo** hairdrier
secar to dry
seco dry
sed f thirst; **tener sed** to be thirsty

segundo second; **segunda clase** second class

seguridad f safety; security

seguro safe, secure; sure

seguro m insurance; **seguro a todo riesgo** comprehensive insurance

sello m stamp

semáforo m traffic light

semana f week; **Semana Santa** Easter, Holy Week

senderismo m walking, hill-walking, hiking; **hacer senderismo** to go walking

sendero m path

sensación f feeling

sensible sensitive

sentarse to sit down

sentido m sense

sentimiento m feeling

sentir to feel; **sentirse bien/mal** to feel good/bad

señal f sign; signal; **señal de tráfico** road sign

Señor Mr

Señora Mrs

Señorita Miss

separar to separate; **separarse** to split up

septiembre m September

ser to be (see grammar)

serio serious

servicio m service; toilet; **servicio de averías** breakdown service; **servicio de caballeros** gents' toilet; **servicio de señoras** ladies' toilet

servilleta f serviette, napkin

sexo m sex

shock m shock

si if; **si no** otherwise, if not

sí yes

siempre always

siesta f nap; **echar una siesta** to have a nap

siglo m century

significar to mean; **¿qué significa?** what does it mean?

siguiente next

silencio m silence

silencioso quiet, silent

silla f chair; **silla de ruedas** wheelchair

sillita f (de ruedas) pushchair

silvestre wild

simpático nice, pleasant

sin without; **sin gas** still, flat

sinagoga f synagogue

sitio m place, spot; **sitio web** website; **en ningún sitio** nowhere; **en todos sitios** everywhere

sobre above; on; **sobre la mesa** on the table

sobre m envelope

socio m, **socia** f member

¡socorro! help!

sol m sun

sólo only

soltero single, not married

sombra shade

sombrero m hat

sombrilla f beach umbrella

somnífero m sleeping pill

sonreír to smile

sonrisa f smile

sordo deaf

sorprender to surprise

sorpresa f surprise

sostener to hold

su, sus his; her; your; their (see grammar)

ubmarinismo *m* scuba diving
ubtitulado subtitled
ucio dirty
udar to sweat
uelo *m* floor; ground
ueño *m* sleep
uerte *f* luck; **tener suerte** to be lucky
uficiente enough
ufrir to suffer
ugerir to suggest
ujetador *m* bra
upermercado *m* supermarket
uplemento *m* extra, additional charge, supplement
upuesto: ¡por supuesto! of course!
ur *m* south
urf: hacer surf to surf, go surfing
urfear to surf, go surfing
urfing *m* surfing
uyo, suya, suyos, suyas his; hers; yours; theirs *(see grammar)*

T

abaco *m* tobacco
abla *f* plank, board; **tabla de surf** surfboard
ajada *f* slice
alla *f* size
amaño *m* size
ambién too, also
ampón *m* tampon
an so; as
apa *f* tapa, snack; cover
apón *m* plug *(bath, sink)*; **tapones para los oídos** earplugs
aquilla *f* ticket office
arde late
arde *f* afternoon; **por la tarde** in the afternoon

tareas *fpl* **domésticas** housework
tarjeta *f* card; **tarjeta de crédito** credit card; **tarjeta de débito** debit card; **tarjeta telefónica** phonecard
taxi *m* taxi
taxista *mf* taxi driver
taza *f* cup
teatro *m* theatre
tejido *m* material
telefonista *mf* switchboard operator
teléfono *m* phone; **teléfono móvil** mobile phone
teleobjetivo *m* zoom lens
telesilla *f* chairlift
telesquí *m* ski lift
televisión *f* television
temperatura *f* temperature
templo *m* temple
temporada *f* season
temporal temporary
temprano early
tendero *m*, **tendera** *f* shopkeeper
tenedor *m* fork
tener to have; **tener que** to have to, must; **tengo que irme** I have to go
tenis *m* tennis
tensión *f* **arterial** blood pressure; **tensión alta** high blood pressure; **tensión baja** low blood pressure
tentempié *m* snack
terminal *f* terminal
terminar to finish
termo *m* Thermos® flask
termómetro *m* thermometer
terraza *f* terrace
terrible terrible
tía *f* aunt
tibio lukewarm

tiempo *m* weather; time; **hace mal tiempo** the weather's bad

tienda *f* shop; tent

tierra *f* earth; soil

tijeras *fpl* scissors

tímido shy

tío *m* uncle; guy, bloke

típico typical

tipo *m* kind, sort, type; **¿qué tipo de …?** what kind of …?; **tipo de cambio** exchange rate

tirar to throw, to throw away; to pull; **tirarse al agua** to dive *(into water)*

tirita *f* sticking plaster, Elastoplast®

toalla *f* towel; **toalla de baño** bath towel

tobillo *m* ankle

tocar to touch

todavía still; yet

todo, toda, todos, todas all; every; **toda la semana** all week; **todo el tiempo** all the time; **todo incluido** all inclusive; **todo el mundo** everybody, everyone; **todo recto** straight ahead, straight on

tomar to take; **tomar el sol** to sunbathe

torcerse to sprain; **torcerse el tobillo** to sprain one's ankle

tormenta *f* storm

tos *f* cough

toser to cough

trabajar to work

trabajo *m* job; work

tradicional traditional

traducir to translate

traer to bring

tráfico *m* traffic

traje *m* suit; **traje de baño** swimsuit; **traje isotérmico** wetsuit

tranquilo calm, quiet

transferencia *f* transfer

tranvía *m* tram

través: a través de across; through

tren *m* train

triste sad

trozo *m* piece, bit, slice

tu your *(see grammar)*

tú you *(see grammar)*

tubo *m* **de escape** exhaust pipe

turista *mf* tourist

turno *m* turn

tuyo, tuya, tuyos, tuyas yours *(see grammar)*

U

un *m*, **una** *f* a; one *(see grammar)*

uña *f* nail, fingernail, toenail

Union *f* **Europea** European Union

urgencia *f* emergency

urgente urgent; express *(letter)*

usar to use

útil useful

V

vacaciones *fpl* holiday(s); **vacaciones organizadas** package holiday

vacío empty

vacunado (contra) vaccinated (against)

¡vale! OK!

valer to be worth; **vale la pena** it's worth it

válido valid

valle *m* valley

varios several

vaso *m* glass

vecino *m*, **vecina** *f* neighbour

vegetariano vegetarian

vela *f* candle

velocidad *f* speed

venda *f* bandage

vendaje *m* bandage

vender to sell

venir to come

venta *f* sale

ventana *f* window

ventilador *m* electric fan

ver to see

verano *m* summer

verdad: es verdad it's true

verdadero true

verde green

verdulería *f* greengrocer's

vergüenza *f* shame; outrage

Vespa® *f* scooter

vestido *m* dress

vestir to dress; **vestirse** to get dressed

vestuario *m* changing room

vez *f* time; **en vez de** instead of; **de vez en cuando** from time to time; **otra vez** again; **a veces** sometimes; **una vez** once; **dos veces** twice

viajar to travel

viaje *m* trip, journey; **viaje de ida** outward journey; **viaje de novios** honeymoon; **viaje de vuelta** return journey; **¡buen viaje!** have a good trip!

vida *f* life

vidriera *f* stained-glass window

viento *m* wind

viernes *m* Friday

vino *m* wine; **vino blanco** white wine; **vino rosado** rosé wine; **vino tinto** red wine

violar to rape

visado *m* visa

visita *f* visit; **visita guiada** guided tour

visitar to visit

vista *f* view; **vista al mar** sea view

vivir to live

vivo alive

volar to fly

voleibol *m* volleyball

volver to return, to come back, to go back

vomitar to vomit

vuelo *m* flight

vuelta *f* return; drive; **dar una vuelta en coche** to go for a drive

WXYZ

walkman® Walkman®, personal stereo

whisky *m* **escocés** scotch

windsurf(ing) *m* windsurfing

y and; **tú y yo** you and I; **las diez y cuarto** a quarter past ten

ya already

yo I

yo mismo *m*, **yo misma** *f* myself

zapatilla *f* **de tenis** tennis shoe

zapato *m* shoe

zona *f* area

zoo *m* zoo

zoológico *m* zoo

zoom *m* zoom lens

zumo *m* juice

GRAMMAR

It is important to **stress** Spanish words correctly; this is easy if you follow these simple rules.

If the word has a written accent, stress the vowel with the accent on it: **fácil, ácido, préstamo, televisión, café**.

If the word has no written accent and ends in a vowel or -n or -s, stress the next-to-last syllable: **bicicleta, trabajo, corte, comen, mesas**.

If the word has no written accent and ends in any consonant <u>except</u> -n or -s, stress the last syllable: **ciudad, final, comer, trabajar**.

Spanish has four ways of saying *you*; it distinguishes between singular and plural, and between the **polite** and **familiar** forms. Use the familiar form when speaking to friends or children, and the polite form to strangers, older people or people in authority. The familiar form (singular **tú**; plural **vosotros**) uses the second person of the verb and the polite form (singular **usted**; plural **ustedes**) uses the third person. Note, though, that the pronoun is not necessary, except for emphasis, as the ending of the verb tells you which person is involved. So, there are four ways to ask *how are you?*, for example:

	Singular	*Plural*
Familiar	¿cómo estás (tú)?	¿cómo estáis (vosotros)?
Polite	¿cómo está (usted)?	¿cómo están (ustedes)?

To convert a statement into a **question** it is sufficient to use a rising intonation at the end of the sentence; there is no change in word order:

viene he's coming, ¿viene? is he coming?
¿quién quiere venir? who wants to come?

To make a sentence **negative**, simply insert no before the verb:

Juan come carne Juan eats meat
Juan no come carne Juan doesn't eat meat

Spanish nouns are either **masculine** or **feminine**. The **definite article** (*the* in English) and **indefinite article** (*a/an* in English) vary according to whether the noun is masculine or feminine and singular or plural:

	Masculine singular	Masculine plural	Feminine singular	Feminine plural
Definite	el	los	la	las
Indefinite	un	unos	una	unas

el chico the boy, los chicos the boys, un chico a boy,
unos chicos some boys
la chica the girl, las chicas the girls, una chica a girl,
unas chicas some girls

The ending of a noun is usually a good indication as to its gender. There are a few exceptions, but most nouns ending in -o are masculine and most ending in -a are feminine:

el año (year), el vaso (glass), el vino (wine),
el desayuno (breakfast)
la semana (week), la taza (cup), la cerveza (beer),
la comida (food/lunch)

Some common exceptions are: el día (day), el problema (problem), el idioma (language), el clima (climate), el mapa (map), la mano (hand), la radio (radio), la foto (photo) and la moto (motorbike).

As for other endings, nouns in -or are masculine: el congelador (freezer), el amor (love); and nouns in -ción, -sión, -tad and -dad are feminine: la estación (station), la ciudad (town, city).

The **plural** of nouns is formed by adding -s if the singular ends in a vowel, and -es if it ends in a consonant:

mesa → mesas (tables), cuchillo → cuchillos (knives)
hotel → hoteles (hotels), tren → trenes (trains)

Note that a final -z changes to -ces in the plural:

una vez (once), dos veces (twice); un pez (a fish),
dos peces (two fishes)

Adjectives in Spanish agree with nouns in number and gender and usually go <u>after</u> the noun:

un vino blanco (a white wine), dos vinos blancos
(two white wines)
una calle estrecha (a narrow street), calles estrechas
(narrow streets)

GRAMMAR

179

In the mini-dictionary in this phrasebook, we give the masculine singular and feminine singular forms of adjectives. The plural of adjectives is formed in the same way as for nouns:

> **bonito, bonita, bonitos, bonitas** (beautiful)
> **caro, cara, caros, caras** (dear, expensive)

Note how the feminine and plural of some other adjectives are formed:

> **inglés, inglesa, ingleses, inglesas** (English)
> **español, española, españoles, españolas** (Spanish)
> **encantador, encantadora, encantadores, encantadoras** (charming)

Possessive adjectives (*my, your, his* etc.) in Spanish are as follows:

> *Singular*   **mi, mis** (my)
>   **tu, tus** (your[1])
>   **su, sus** (his, her, its, your[2])
> *Plural*   **nuestro, nuestra, nuestros, nuestras** (our)
>   **vuestro, vuestra, vuestros, vuestras** (your[1])
>   **su, sus** (their, your[2])

[1] Familiar form of address. [2] Polite form of address.

Note particularly that Spanish does not distinguish between *his* and *her* – **su/sus** is used for both – and that **su/sus** is also used to translate *your* when using the polite form of address. While all possessive adjectives have a plural form, only **nuestro/a** and **vuestro/a** have separate feminine forms.

> **mi hermano** (my brother) **mis hermanas** (my sisters)
> **nuestro piso** (our flat), **nuestras novias** (our girlfriends)
> **su casa** (his/her/their/your house)

Most **adverbs** are formed by taking the feminine singular form of the adjective and adding -**mente**:

> **perfecto → perfectamente** (perfectly)

Some common adverbs not formed in this way are **bien** (well) and **mal** (badly).

Note that **subject pronouns** (*I, you, we* etc.) are generally not required in Spanish, except for emphasis, because the ending of the verb indicates who the subject is. It is enough to say, for example: **voy** (I go), **vamos** (we go), **van** (they go), etc.

yo (I)	nosotros/nosotras (we)
tú (you[1])	vosotros/vosotras (you[1])
él (he), ella (she), usted (you[2])	ellos/ellas (they), ustedes (you[2])

[1] Familiar form of address. [2] Polite form of address.

There is no single equivalent of *it*; use **él** or **ella** depending on the gender of the noun.

Spanish pronouns may seem more complex than in English; for example, you must distinguish between direct object and indirect object pronouns in the third person:

Direct object	**lo** vi ayer (I saw **him** yesterday)
	la vi hace una semana (I saw **her** a week ago)
Indirect object	**le** di un regalo (I gave **him/her** a present)
	le pedí un cigarro (I asked **him/her** for a cigarette)

Note that you must insert the preposition **a** before the direct object when the direct object is a person:

conocen a Pedro (they know Pedro)

Remember also that a different form is used after a preposition in the first and second person singular:

te he traído un regalo I have brought you a present
tengo un regalo para **ti** I have a present for you

For reference, here is the table of subject, object and reflexive pronouns:

	Subject	Direct object	Indirect object	After preposition	Reflexive
Singular	yo	me	me	mí	me
	tú	te	te	ti	te
	él	lo	le	él	se
	ella	la	le	ella	se
	usted	lo/la	le	usted	se
Plural	nosotros/as	nos	nos	nosotros/as	nos
	vosotros/as	os	os	vosotros/as	os
	ellos	los	les	ellos	se
	ellas	las	les	ellas	se
	ustedes	los/las	les	ustedes	se

Possessive pronouns are words like *mine*, *hers*, *yours* and *ours*, as in this example:

> este asiento es **el mío**, **el tuyo** es ese (this seat is **mine**, **yours** is that one)

Here is the list for reference.
(el) mío, (la) mía, (los) míos, (las) mías (mine)
(el) tuyo, (la) tuya, (los) tuyos, (las) tuyas (yours[1])
(el) suyo, (la) suya, (los) suyos, (las) suyas (his, hers, yours[2])
(el) nuestro, (la) nuestra, (los) nuestros, (las) nuestras (ours)
(el) vuestro, (la) vuestra, (los) vuestros, (las) vuestras (yours[1])
(el) suyo, (la) suya, (los) suyos, (las) suyas (theirs, yours[2])
[1] Familiar form of address. [2] Polite form of address.

Reflexive verbs are used when the subject and the object of a verb are the same person, and they are constructed with **reflexive pronouns** (see above – in English *myself*, *yourself* etc.). These reflexive pronouns are not always free-standing; they are tagged onto infinitives, imperatives and gerunds, so in the mini-dictionary reflexive verbs all end in -se, eg acordarse (to remember).

> me compré un vestido nuevo (I bought **myself** a new dress)
> se sentó y empezó a comer (he sat **himself** down and started to eat)

However, they are much more common in Spanish, and do not always translate into English with a -*self* pronoun because English often expresses the idea differently:

> me levanto, me ducho y me visto (I get up, I have a shower and I get dressed)
> ¡lávate, aféitate y vístete! (get washed, have a shave and get dressed!)

In other cases it might not be so clear why a Spanish verb is reflexive:

> nos conocimos en una fiesta (we met at a party)
> se marcharon sin decir adiós (they left without saying goodbye)
> no me acuerdo de su nombre (I don't remember her name)

Spanish **verbs** are divided into three groups (conjugations), ending in -ar, -er and -ir.

GRAMMAR

Here is the present tense of three regular verbs, one from each conjugation. A hyphen has been inserted only so that you can see the endings more clearly:

hablar	comer	vivir
habl-**o**	com-**o**	viv-**o**
habl-**as**	com-**es**	viv-**es**
habl-**a**	com-**e**	viv-**e**
habl-**amos**	com-**emos**	viv-**imos**
habl-**áis**	com-**éis**	viv-**ís**
habl-**an**	com-**en**	viv-**en**

habla usted muy bien español you speak very good Spanish
no como carne I don't eat meat
¿dónde vives? where do you live?

Irregular verbs undergo certain spelling changes, which you will have to learn. Here are some common irregular verbs in the present tense:

tener (to have)	**ir** (to go)	**querer** (to want)
tengo	voy	quiero
tienes	vas	quieres
tiene	va	quiere
tenemos	vamos	queremos
tenéis	vais	queréis
tienen	van	quieren

venir (to come)	**haber** (to have)	**poder** (can)
vengo	he	puedo
vienes	has	puedes
viene	ha	puede
venimos	hemos	podemos
venís	habéis	podéis
vienen	han	pueden

Note that **haber** is also an auxiliary verb and can be used to form the present perfect tense:

he comprado un pantalón (I've bought some trousers)
¿has visto esta película? (have you seen this film?)
no hemos comido nada (we haven't eaten anything)

Some verbs are irregular only in the first person singular:
hacer (to do, to make): **hago**, haces, hace …
saber (to know – something): **sé**, sabes, sabe …
conocer (to know – someone): **conozco**, conoces, conoce …

Note there are two Spanish verbs which translate the English *to be*, **ser** and **estar**. The basic difference between the two is that **ser** describes permanent states and inherent qualities, whereas **estar** describes temporary situations and geographical location. Here is the present tense of both:

> **ser**: soy, eres, es, somos, sois, son
> **estar**: estoy, estás, está, estamos, estáis, están

> es inglés (he's English)
> su mujer es alta (his wife is tall)
> están de vacaciones (they're on holiday)
> el hotel está cerca de la playa (the hotel is near the beach)

The **imperfect** of regular verbs is as follows. This tense is used to denote a continuous action in the past (eg I **was talking** to him). Note that -er and -ir verbs have the same endings:

hablar	comer	vivir
habl-**aba**	com-**ía**	viv-**ía**
habl-**abas**	com-**ías**	viv-**ías**
habl-**aba**	com-**ía**	viv-**ía**
habl-**ábamos**	com-**íamos**	viv-**íamos**
habl-**abais**	com-**íais**	viv-**íais**
habl-**aban**	com-**ían**	viv-**ían**

estar is regular in the imperfect; **ser** is conjugated as follows:
> era, eras, era, éramos, erais, eran

The **past simple** of regular verbs is as follows. This tense is used to denote a single action, or an action seen as short, in the past (eg I **saw** him yesterday).

Note that -**er** and -**ir** verbs have the same endings:

hablar	comer	vivir
habl-**é**	com-**í**	viv-**í**
habl-**aste**	com-**iste**	viv-**iste**
habl-**ó**	com-**ió**	viv-**ió**
habl-**amos**	com-**imos**	viv-**imos**
habl-**asteis**	com-**isteis**	viv-**isteis**
habl-**aron**	com-**ieron**	viv-**ieron**

Notice how these two tenses are used:

llovía fuerte, así que cogí mi paraguas
it was raining hard so I took my umbrella
caminaba por el bosque cuando empezó a llover
I was walking through the forest when it started to rain
antes vivía en el campo
I used to live in the country
viví tres meses en Madrid
I lived in Madrid for three months

The past simple of **ser** and **estar** are as follows:

ser: fui, fuiste, fue, fuimos, fuisteis, fueron
estar: estuve, estuviste, estuvo, estuvimos, estuvisteis, estuvieron

To form the future tense, simply add the following endings onto the infinitive:

-**é**, -**ás**, -**á**, -**emos**, -**éis**, -**án**.
hablar : hablaré, hablarás, hablará, hablaremos, hablaréis, hablarán

hablaré con él mañana (I'll talk to him tomorrow)
el autocar llegará en seguida (the coach will arrive shortly)

HOLIDAYS AND FESTIVALS

NATIONAL BANK HOLIDAYS

In Spain, bank holidays are known as **días festivos**. Administrativ departments, banks, offices and most shops are closed, but most bar restaurants, museums and other tourist attractions remain open (albeit wi restricted opening hours). Apart from national holidays, autonomous region and towns and cities also have their own holidays when shops and ban close

1 January	**día de Año Nuevo** (New Year's Day)
6 January	**Día de los Reyes Magos** (Epiphany)
March/April	**Viernes Santo** (Good Friday)
1 May	**Fiesta del Trabajo** (Labour Day)
15 August	**Asunción** (Assumption)
12 October	**Día de la Hispanidad** (National Day, Columbus Day)
1 November	**Día de todos los Santos** (All Saints' Day)
6 December	**Día de la Constitución** (Constitution Day)
8 December	**Inmaculada Concepción** (Immaculate Conception)
25 December	**Navidad** (Christmas Day)

FESTIVALS

There always seems to be a festival going on somewhere in Spain. Many traditional religious festivals are still observed, but all the celebrations are an opportunity to have a good time. In summer, every village has its own festival. Here a just a few of the best-known and most impressive:

February	Carnivals are held all over Spain. The **carnaval de Cádiz** and the **carnaval de Tenerife** (in the Canary Islands) are without a doubt the most famous in Spain. In Cádiz groups of musicians known as **chirigotas** parade through the streets, portraying the year's major social, cultural and

political events through satirical songs, which are specially written for the occasion. The **carnaval de Tenerife** runs throughout February and its exuberant mood is reminiscent of Brazil's famous Rio Carnival. A different theme is chosen each year, and locals vie with each other to see who can create the most elaborate costumes. The **carnaval de Sitges** (on the Catalonian coast) is on a much smaller scale, but has a reputation for being one of the wildest.

March

For **Valencia**'s famous **Fallas**, locals can spend months building huge papier-maché statues, which are often satirical references to current affairs. However, all but one of them are burnt on the **Nit del foc** (night of fire), which ends this celebration known for its fireworks.

March–April

Besides Christmas, **Semana Santa** (Holy Week or Easter Week) is the largest and most important national holiday in Spain. People line the streets to see the processions of religious brotherhoods and their floats with statues of Christ or the Virgin Mary (carried by **costaleros**, who support the vast weight on their shoulders) followed by the penitents (**penitentes**) dressed in long black or purple robes and pointed hats. The most famous processions are those held in **Sevilla**, **Valladolid**, **Zamora**, **Murcia** and **Cuenca**.

April

The **Feria de Sevilla** (also known as the **Feria de abril**) is held exactly two weeks after Holy Week, and is just as impressive to watch. The residents of Seville dress up in traditional costume to dance the **sevillana**, sing and parade through the streets on horseback.

Pentecost
(7th Sunday after Easter)

For the **romería de Rocío** (the pilgrimage to Rocío), the people of Andalusia dress up in traditional costume and ride to the small village of **El**

Rocío on horseback, accompanied by processions of elaborately-decorated wagons pulled by cattle. Every year, almost a million visitors follow the procession of the Virgin of Rocío through the village streets.

June

San Juan (St John's Day, 24 June). Throughout Catalonia and the Mediterranean region bonfires are lit and fireworks let off on the night of the 23rd to celebrate the summer solstice, the shortest night of the year. On Menorca there are various festivals and events involving horses.

July

The town of **Pamplona** holds the week-long **San Fermin** festival, which begins at twelve noon on 6 July with the launching of a rocket, known as the **chupinazo**, from the balcony of the town hall. At eight in the morning for the next eight days, the bulls which are to be fought in the evening are driven from their pens outside the city walls, through the streets to the bullring, a distance of 825 metres. In these **encierros**, crowds of daring young people run before or along with the bulls and try to avoid mishap.

USEFUL ADDRESSES

British Embassy
/ Fernando el Santo 16
3010 Madrid
l.: 91 700 82 00 or 91 319 02 00
x: 91 700 82 72

British Consulate-General
seo de Recoletos 7/9, 4°
3004 Madrid
l.: 91 524 97 00
x: 91 524 97 30

r details of other consular offices and information in general, visit the
nbassy's website: http://www.ukinspain.com/english/

Irish Embassy
eland House
seo de la Castellana 46, 4°
3046 Madrid
l.: 91 436 40 93
x: 91 435 16 77

r consular offices visit: http://foreignaffairs.gov.ie/embassies/display.asp

American Embassy
rrano 75
3006 Madrid
l.: 91 587 22 00
x: 91 587 23 03

r consular offices visit: http://madrid.usembassy.gov/cons/offices.html

Canadian Embassy
Goya Building
Núñez de Balboa 35
28001 Madrid
Tel.: 91 423 32 50
Fax: 91 423 32 51

For consular offices visit the Embassy's website: http://www.international.
gc.ca/canadaeuropa/spain/embassy-en.asp

Spanish Tourist Office
UK: PO Box 4009, London W1A 6NB
             Tel.: 0207 4868077
Republic of Ireland: PO Box 10015, Dublin 1

For further details visit www.tourspain.co.uk

For details of Spanish Tourist Offices in the US, visit http://www.okspain.
org/quicklinks/offices.asp

For Canada, visit http://www.tourspain.toronto.on.ca

24-hour brochure request line
UK: 08459 400 180
Republic of Ireland: 0818 220 290

The number to ring in an emergency in Spain is **112**.

CONVERSION TABLES

Note that when writing numbers, Spanish uses a comma where English uses a full stop. For example 0.6 would be written 0,6 in Spanish.

Measurements

Only the metric system is used in Spain.

Length
1 cm ≈ 0.4 inches
30 cm ≈ 1 foot

Distance
1 metre ≈ yard
1 km ≈ 0.6 miles

To convert kilometers into miles, divide by 8 and then multiply by 5.

kilometers	1	2	5	10	20	100
miles	0.6	1.25	3.1	6.25	12.50	62.5

To convert miles into kilometers, divide by 5 and then multiply by 8.

miles	1	2	5	10	20	100
kilometers	1.6	3.2	8	16	32	160

Weight
25g ≈ 1 oz   1 kg ≈ 2 lb   6 kg ≈ 1 stone

To convert kilos into pounds, divide by 5 and then multiply by 11.
To convert pounds into kilos, multiply by 5 and then divide by 11.

kilos	1	2	10	20	60	80
pounds	2.2	4.4	22	44	132	176

Liquid
1 litre ≈ 2 pints
5 litres ≈ 1 gallon

Temperature

To convert temperatures in Fahrenheit into Celsius, subtract 32, multiply by 5 and then divide by 9.

To convert temperatures in Celsius into Fahrenheit, divide by 5, multiply by 9 and then add 32.

Fahrenheit (°F)	32	40	50	59	68	86	100
Celsius (°C)	0	4	10	15	20	30	38

Clothes sizes

Sometimes you will find sizes given using the English-language abbreviations **XS** (Extra Small), **S** (Small), **M** (Medium), **L** (Large) and **XL** (Extra Large).

• Women's clothes

Europe	36	38	40	42	44	etc
UK	8	10	12	14	16	

• Bras (cup sizes are the same)

Europe	70	75	80	85	90	etc
UK	32	34	36	38	40	

• Men's shirts (collar size)

Europe	36	38	41	43	etc
UK	14	15	16	17	

• Men's clothes

Europe	40	42	44	46	48	50	etc
UK	30	32	34	36	38	40	

Shoe sizes

• Women's shoes

Europe	37	38	39	40	42	etc
UK	4	5	6	7	8	

• Men's shoes

Europe	40	42	43	44	46	etc
UK	7	8	9	10	11	